HOW TO START YOUR OWN TEA ROOM AND VICTORIAN GIFT GALLERY – FROM A - Z

English Tea Room & Victorian Gift Gallery

"YOUR STEP-BY-STEP GUIDE TO SUCCESS"

By
Joyce Ann Whitaker And Charles J. Whitaker

First published by AuthorHouse 07/20/04

ISBN: 1-4184-6423-6 (e-book)
ISBN: 1-4184-2842-6 (Paperback)

Printed in the United States of America
Bloomington, IN

This book is printed on acid free paper.

The Advisor Group of Companies

> **"Dedicated to helping entrepreneurs to free themselves from job insecurity"**

Dear Entrepreneur:

On behalf of The Advisor Group, Ltd. and the authors, we would like to personally thank you for purchasing this business guide.

A tremendous amount of research, experience and money has gone into this project, and we know for a fact that if you read this business guide and then follow its guidelines, you will increase your chances of running a successful business. This manual is based on practical application, day-to-day experience and valuable lessons learned by the authors as they built a Victorian Gift Gallery and an English Tea Room from scratch beginning in 1994.

The contents of this manual may discourage you from establishing your own business, while others of you will feel capable of duplicating our program. We feel that anyone starting a business of this type may be able to save thousands of dollars and avoid costly mistakes that may not have been avoided without this manual.

Because we have invested well over $850,000 into our business, have learned valuable lessons and have experienced unique circumstances that could help others, we do not offer a refund, except as the state laws of Ohio require. This manual is for the use of the purchaser and is not to be copied, all or in part, or reproduced or disseminated for others' use.

If you are seriously considering starting a tea room and/or gift gallery, you may also wish to take advantage of our consulting fee offered to purchasers of this guide. You would receive personal input to further save you money and assist you in getting your business off to a sound start.

Thank you again for your order. May we suggest you turn the page and get started? There is a great opportunity waiting for you because of the tremendous growth ahead for the tea industry in America.

Joyce & Charles Whitaker, Authors

ABOUT THE AUTHORS

The owners of The Victorian Painted Lady, LLC, Tea Room and Gift Gallery have personally experienced owning and running the business for over ten years. We have faced every obstacle (*"Murphy's Law"*) that a business owner can face.

Joyce Anne Whitaker was a house wife for 20 years before she began her career. She quickly excelled within a very few years, becoming vice president of a national firm and later became the chief marketing officer for the 12th largest privately held company in Chicago. Later she took a job in New York's Wall Street District where she served as vice president providing PR and marketing services to such firms as the Templeton Funds, Fred Alger Management and numerous other financial institutions. Joyce has won several awards during her 18 year career as a financial writer and public relations consultant.

Charles J. Whitaker has served the financial service industry since 1972. In the early 1980s he and Joyce provided business planning, marketing consulting and training to national broker dealers, financial service companies and financial planners. In the late 80s Mr. Whitaker became assistant vice president of MONY in New York where he served as national director of retirement planning, marketing and training for MONY serving their agencies on a national basis. Mr. Whitaker has provided business consulting to many types of businesses over the past years and is qualified to assist anyone in developing their business plan to **start a new business**.

For more information on Mr. Whitaker's background, you may go to his web site at www. advisor-group-ltd.com

ABOUT THIS GUIDE

Our research is based on our personal experiences in Ohio. However, your requirements may be different from those presented in this guide. You may request our business consulting to assist you in localizing your business plan and to help identify variables in your locality.

Although The Advisor Group, Ltd. considers the information in this guide reliable, reporting inaccuracies can occur; consequently, any reader using this information does so at his or her own choosing. People and companies mentioned herein are believed to be reputable, but neither The Advisor Group, Ltd., nor the authors, nor any employees accept responsibility for the activities of those mentioned.

Recognizing that all business opportunities contain certain inherent risks, we suggest that the entrepreneur and any related investors consult with an attorney, and/or accountant with regard to your own local personal investment criteria. This guide is sold with the understanding that the publisher is not engaged in rendering legal or tax advice. If legal advice is required, the services of an attorney should be sought.

THE PUBLISHER

TABLE OF CONTENTS

HISTORICAL PERSPECTIVE

My biography…
"How I started a
Victorian gift gallery
and
English tea room
from scratch."

"10 years in business and still learning."

My autobiography outlines my professional career

and the experience of owning my own business.

This report will help anyone planning to start their own business

and particularly those dreaming of opening a tea room and gift gallery.

Joyce Ann Whitaker

"Starting
your own business"

My Autobiography...
"How I Started A Gift Gallery And Tea Room From Scratch!"

Dedication

This report is dedicated to women who would like to own their own business but don't know where to begin. It is offered to women who often have little business experience, but would love to free themselves from the glass ceiling of corporate America. I hope to assist those who have a dream to free themselves from a male dominated world where women make about 75 percent of the wages men make doing the same or more responsible jobs.

Some women do not have the background and/or experience needed to start their own business. Others have in depth business experience, which makes them better equipped to launch their own business. If running and operating a Victorian gift shop and English tea room sounds exciting to you, then please allow me to guide you.

This report is dedicated specifically to those who are considering starting their own tea room or gift gallery or both. What I have to say may discourage you or it could excite you; whatever its affects on you, my intent is to help you decide whether to proceed into your own business. I will inform you of the good and the bad of operating a tea room and gift gallery.

I wish you the best as you ponder owning your own business. Don't let others destroy your dreams or discourage you, but don't jump into your own business blindly without an experienced person to guide you as a mentor. This single step could save you thousands of dollars, the embarrassment of business failure and maybe help you become a more successful business owner.

Preface

Today, more than ever, Americans are in a quandary over their future because of the uncertainty of the economy. The threats of terrorism and war in Iraq, coupled with corporate scandals and bankruptcies have left many working Americans unsure of their future and bewildered about where their career is headed. Corporate executives have a general lack of concern for employees and only care about profits that keep their salaries and bonuses up and their shareholders happy. Never has there been a better time to start your own business.

My story is a first hand account of what I have experienced during my work history and the obstacles I faced trying to build a business in Marysville, Ohio. This report on **My autobiography…"How I started a Victorian gift gallery and English tea room from scratch"** will detail the trials and tribulations of being an entrepreneur. Even with my years of corporate experience as an executive and my personal business experience, I still was shocked at the obstacles I faced as my business evolved over the past ten years. Yes, I made costly mistakes and I have learned a lot of tough lessons during my pilgrimage, yet what I learned from these lessons can be very beneficial to others planning a new venture.

Always remember, no business is easy to operate! If you are considering setting up your own tea room and/or a gift gallery, understand that you also will make costly mistakes unless you have a mentor who can consult with you as you step into this new arena of owning your own business. Just think how many times Thomas Edison failed at making a light bulb, or Benjamin Franklin's attempts to discover electricity or the failures of Eli Whitney as he attempted to invent the cotton gin. Yes, you know for certain that you will make costly mistakes and face numerous business "surprises" when you start your own business.

If running your own business was easy, everyone would be doing it and there would be no profit in doing so. Unless you are a "tough cookie," are determined and have tenacity, don't even think about starting your own business without a mentor or consultant. **Launching a new business will have financial surprises 100 percent of the time.** You will not avoid them even if you have years of experience in the exact business you are considering.

Many women have come to me to pick my brain on how to run a tea room. Two ladies came to me for advice and were unwilling to pay me a consulting fee, saying they could do it alone. They were open only one year and went out of business. On the other hand, I charged an hourly rate to consult with a woman from New York and she is still thriving. Sadly, others have thought, "It would be fun to run a tea room."

They start out naively with good intentions and a dream, never realizing the requirements, financial and otherwise, long hours and hard work involved. To succeed your business must be like a marriage with the same passion, commitment and dedication.

We have had corporate executives of restaurant chains visit our tea room to gain insight of our operation. Our unique approach has gained media attention and popularity. Many have tried to get ideas for their own business, but what most of these folks don't realize is there is more to it than what you see during a single visit. Most of the knowledge is in my head. I have a unique gift of intuition, coordination and design ability.

My business skills and over 30 years experience as an executive in varied businesses and the corporate world gives me a broad range of knowledge from which to draw. Importantly, I failed at one business before I started my Victorian gift store, which taught me the biggest lessons of all. Very few people have the skill to start and run a business without the help of a consultant who has experience in their planned venture. Yet, with all of my training, it has been tough to make the business profitable. There will always be variables such as the economy, competition and trends. What you must do is be willing to make the necessary adjustments to survive.

Introduction

My humble beginning... I will share with you my background in the business and executive world and later my struggle to survive in my own business. These experiences helped set the stage for my future career and business endeavors.

I married at age 17, just two months after high school graduation in 1959. In the fifties girls in my family were taught to get married and rear a family. Career choices were not as varied as today. You married forever, regardless of how unhappy you were. I was too young to be married and as many women did in my day, I stuck it out. By age 19, I gave birth to my first child, a son. I made a choice to be a good mother and I truly loved motherhood. By age 25 I had two sons and a daughter. For the next few years, I reveled in my children. When the children began school, I became very involved in scouts, school activities and chaired many fund raising events, always working for no pay, just self gratification and filling a need.

My first dream of owning a business was in the sixties. I designed a portfolio of plus sized women's clothing and wanted to open a retail store. I had page after page of drawings and research. I had been assured by a company in Texas that they would back me if I could buy $10,000 worth of merchandise from them up front. When I discussed my dream with my husband, he totally refused and did nothing but laugh at me…he said I was crazy and I could never run a business. That was my first tough business experience. The frustrating part was that this was even before Lane Bryant and other plus sized clothing stores were even begun. I would have been at the forefront of the industry. I even went to our local bank with my business plan for a personal loan. Our bank said my husband had to sign for the loan, which was only $10,000. He refused. From then on I kept my ideas quiet and filled folders with designs and ideas. I was totally suppressed, but I was still dreaming quietly. (I became an entrepreneur 20 years later!)

I became a Welcome Wagon hostess for my community when my youngest child started to kindergarten. I enjoyed this low paying job because it exposed me to newcomers, businesses and sponsors in our community. I did this for a few years until my youngest was ten years old. Then, out of the blue, I became pregnant with my fourth child. This was devastating to me because I was planning to separate from my husband in the spring. I had complications in my pregnancy and had to give up my hostess job, which was very hard to do. I thought about an abortion but simply could not do it. I agonized over my decision, then resolved to do what I had always done…be the best mother I knew how to be.

After nearly twenty years of an abusive first marriage I began laying plans for a divorce. My sons were approaching graduation and I then felt I could handle the girls financially. I was so unhappy and was so tired of being mentally and physically abused that I could no longer endure my marriage. One afternoon as I sat in my backyard with my two year old daughter I prayed for God to find me something to do, something just for me! God answered my prayer. The very next day one of my previous Welcome Wagon sponsors (the president of the bank) called and asked me to come in for an interview for a new program they were starting. To make a long story short, he offered me the position and I went home to discuss this with my husband. He flat out said no. To my husband's dismay, I took the job anyway. My prayer had been answered. When my baby daughter was two I went back to work with serious feelings of guilt. You see, I had never had a babysitter for any of my children and I cherished my little princess.

My first husband, a domineering man of five foot nine, said I could never make it without him. Needless to say, my salary the first year was more than he had earned annually his whole life. I am not putting him down, but he had had several offers for promotion but would never take any risks…he would not move, didn't want responsibility and could never handle accountability…but he surely could criticize, put people down and belittle everyone around him, including any thought I ever had about opening a business.

I quickly excelled at my new position, which meant the end of my marriage. My first husband was totally threatened. I begged him to get counseling and asked him to let me go with his blessing, let me do something for me. He said, "If anybody is going to change it's going to be you because I am happy and there is nothing wrong with me." It was as if a switch clicked in my head. That was the end. I was finished with our marriage. He was not going to work with me, he had lost control of me and had become more violent. I moved out on my own taking the girls with me.

All those warnings from my husband had been proven wrong. I was successful. My first marriage ended, which marked the beginning of finding myself. Finally, I was utilizing the God given talents that I had suppressed for so long. I was headed for the corporate world. Many times I was scared underneath, but I kept trying and never let it show. Little did I know at the time that I could excel in a man's world without a college degree. Yes, you may be surprised but **I do not have a college degree.** The only college education I have is two writing classes I took at a Miami University branch where I lived.

I became strong by taking risks. I will share with you the foundation that was laid to help me excel in the business and executive world and later in my own business. These background experiences helped set the stage for my future career.

My Career Path

The position at the bank resulted in three promotions in four years. I launched the **"in home banking"** program bringing in over a million dollars of new money to the bank. My efforts resulted in several new trust accounts. All was going well until my superior felt threatened. He said the program needed a more experienced banker to take over the program (I was getting too much attention). I was "promoted" to new accounts and doubled as a marketing assistant to the marketing director. Happily, life gave me lemons and I again made lemonade. From then on, marketing and public relations was my forte'. I loved the creativity. I named and designed new bank products and services and handled all the promotions. A *"Hometown Holiday"* celebration I helped create won a bank marketing award and the program has become a tradition.

During my career at the bank I was offered a position at a financial planning association that offered marketing and public relations support services to financial planners in over 25 states and Puerto Rico. There I served as vice president. My responsibilities were consulting with financial planning offices across the country assisting them in public relations and marketing. I designed and wrote brochures, communications and gained publicity through the media. During my tenure with the association, I conducted 12 national public relations and marketing seminars around the country to assist in recruiting new members. This public relations and marketing experience gave me the confidence I needed to market any business. Marketing and public relations is one of the most important business "hats" any business owner can wear if their business is to succeed.

One example of a unique public relations event was the development of a "financial fair" for one financial planner in Carlyle, Ohio. I organized and promoted this event as a "financial fair" to the local media. The event consisted of broker exhibitors in his barn, a tent for meetings, a national speaker and a drawing for prizes. A balloon ride was the major event, which drew hundreds of people and media attention. The event was featured on the front cover of *Financial Planning Magazine*, the industry's top publication.

However, that was not the main event. As a result of this publicity, I met my current husband. Seeing the balloon picture on the front of *Financial Planning Magazine* and reading the feature article, Charles "Chuck" Whitaker, the owner of Registered Financial Planning, Inc. from Oregon called and flew to Ohio to learn more about our services.

That year I was chosen as "the most outstanding employee" of the association winning its top award. I was recognized in the annual meeting and given a $500 bonus. As usual when you go up, you must come down…A group of members of the association at the next year's annual event tried to get the president to vote me in on the all male board of directors. This promotion on my behalf and my relationship with my current husband was the beginning of the downfall of my business relationship with the president. His face became blood red when the members tried to promote me and he was intimidated by my fiance'. Frankly, I think he wanted total control over me because I made him look good to the board and to the company members. For whatever reason, I was later fired.

Getting fired was a shock. I loved my work and had given 100 percent to my job. I brought national attention to the association, gained new members and within one year helped it to grow far beyond its previous level of success. After I left the company, it went down hill within a short time. The board and the members knew that I was the key to providing the public relations and marketing services in the field and slowly but surely they began leaving. Many of them told me they left because of my being fired. One lady said when you left the heart was gone…it was never the same!

The next step in helping other businesses to succeed was when I joined my husband to form a marketing company in 1984, The Advisor Group, Ltd. This helped us start a national consulting company serving the financial services industry. During this career move we helped financial service companies get radio programs started, helped broker dealers design corporate brochures and helped financial services offices develop and promote themselves in order to grow their businesses. This experience further advanced my skills to help others succeed.

During mid-year of 1985 I faced another career change. I was offered a position with a big company in Chicago. They flew me there for an interview. The company was the tenth largest privately held corporation in Chicago and had 12 different companies in its conglomerate. They owned a bank, real estate management company, rental and commercial properties, a broker dealership and other businesses.

My interview with the president and 90 percent owner of the company went exceptionally well. He was interviewing me to take over their public relations and marketing department and my challenge was to centralize all of the companies' marketing programs into one public relations, marketing and communications department. The offer was exciting, but I had to have the president's commitment that he would back me as I dealt with the "egos" of each company president. He gave me that commitment and I took the job and moved to Chicago in November of 1985. I was now vice president in charge of communications.

During the many challenges I faced, the president was true to his word and backed me when one of the company presidents refused to cooperate. He gave me the strong hand I needed as a woman to get the job done. Because of his support my department was able to handle all public relations and marketing for his companies, which saved over $300,000 the first year. This was the most exciting career I have ever had, and I was very well compensated.

However, again I had to make a choice. My fiancé took a great position in New York and moved. He gave me an ultimatum to marry him by March. To me love was more powerful than a good job. I am sharing this information only because I walked away from this position to move to New York to be married (my second marriage). In New York I took a vice president's position of a corporation in the print district of Manhattan where I developed and worked with major financial accounts in the Wall Street District.

One day I found that the president was unethical (I won't go into details). He asked me to have breakfast with him at the *"Windows of the World"* at the top of the World Trade Center. During our breakfast meeting he asked me, ***"How much will it cost to keep you on the job?"*** and I replied, ***"You can't pay me enough to stay!"*** He then asked me another question, ***"How much will it cost me to keep you from suing me?"*** and I thought about it a while and then told him I would not sue him if he gave me $5,000. He opened his check book and wrote me a $5,000 check and that was the end of my position with his company. I was looking over his shoulder and could see the Statue of Liberty standing proudly in the bay. As I watched the sunlight sparkling on the skyscrapers below, I had never felt so empowered. I took the check, took the elevator to the bottom floor and cashed the check at my bank…Chase Manhattan.

I then called my husband who was assistant vice president of MONY Financial Services and told him I have some good news and some bad news. He said what happened? I told him I had quit my job and that I was going shopping in Manhattan. He simply said, "I expected it. Have fun!" I was FREE!

That day was one of the best days I had ever encountered. It was a true beginning for me. No longer would I ever allow a man or boss to dominate my life. I shopped for a while, then had lunch at one of Manhattan's famous restaurants. As I sat there with reality facing me, (you see I had just resigned from a very good paying job), I started to plan my future. My first plan was to make a few calls to successful people I had worked with in the past on various projects. My creativity had always been my real strength and my people skills were well honed after being in management for so many years. Virtually every experience I had had in the past had been basic training for running my own business in the future. For several years I worked as a marketing communications and public relations consultant to Wall Street financial firms and investment companies and brokers

One day an announcement was spotted in the Wall Street Journal that MONY was downsizing. The article went on to say that $75,000 million dollars would be cut from the budget and that 75 percent of the cuts would come from middle management. What a shock! My husband was traveling all over America helping various MONY offices provide educational employee benefits programs as a retirement planning service to large companies. Now he would have to face a career decision as Arthur Anderson was hired to do an internal study of all departments. The Human Resource Department conducted meetings telling us what was going on and a corporate attorney was always present. The fact is that MONY wanted to downsize and was using fear tactics to create a voluntary reduction in force by scaring people into leaving. My husband was not so lucky. He was fired because he loved his work and was not going to quit.

Even though he had conducted national human resource seminars in seven cities around the country presenting the retirement planning program he developed, his position was not seen as a priority. Even though he had clients such as NASA Space Flight Center engineers in Huntsville, Alabama, New Jersey Institute of Technology, Martin Marietta Corporation, Monroe Auto Equipment Company and many others, the company saw his marketing efforts as an expense. So another good executive had lost his career due to downsizing, re-engineering, reduction in force, age discrimination or whatever you want to call this workplace phenomena!

What would we do next? My whole family was in Ohio…mother, children and grandchildren. I decided I wanted to move back to Ohio to be near them.

My husband and I talked and we agreed to make the move back to Ohio so I could be near my mother who was in her 70s at the time. Even though I could take my consulting clients with me and he had a generous severance package, we basically had to begin anew. We had loved New York and liked living there, but executive jobs were scarce at the time and the cost of living was double to living in Ohio. We believed we had made a sound strategic decision.

Getting work in Ohio was difficult after having worked in New York. We both had high salaries, great positions and large departments that we had managed. We had several interviews but were not hired because of the standard "You are over qualified." or "Your salary is too high." To make a long story short, I kept consulting and my husband started his own financial planning practice.

At least one of us expected to find a career in Columbus Ohio but, we were both nearly age 49 at the time and little did we realize that health care costs, high income and over qualification would prevent either of us from finding a career. We never got a chance to find work in Ohio because no one responded to our excellent resumes. Another fact we did not realize was that corporate America was radically downsizing management levels of the corporate management model. The "middle" management was being eliminated. We were both victims of corporate America's downsizing, reduction in force, age discrimination and re-engineering or whatever you want to call the demoralizing of the American workforce. Corporate America was switching to hiring cheaper labor to compete in world markets and was hiring the younger baby boom population and investing in training to keep labor costs down, reduce health care costs and minimize the older populations pension and retiree benefits costs. Older Americans were being discriminated against in favor of younger boomer workers.

Following many attempts to find an executive level position, I decided to try my hand at starting a city magazine. My writing and design skills could be used for this new venture. The magazine was very well done and the Chamber, City Offices and other groups wanted me to provide free magazines for those who had interest in our area. Never once did these groups support us by running ads or funding special promotions. In fact, it was the opposite, they seemed to eagerly want us to fail.

I published *Dublin Magazine* single-handedly for two years. I developed the format, sold advertising, wrote and managed the publication. Although it was a popular, beautiful magazine that won a Bronze Quill Award for Excellence in publishing, I burned out after seven issues. I had serious money problems. I was totally under funded and I had been over charged by a designer and printer. At the end I found the resources that would have allowed my magazine to be profitable, but it was too late. I had to dissolve the publication. It broke my heart after working day and night for two years.

A few years later, the City of Dublin has copied my magazine concept by producing a glitzy magazine well financed by city funds. *Now it is their idea and the money flows freely.*

For a while I was really down, then I worked with my husband for several years. I was fulfilling his dream, but I was restless and hated the technical nature of finances. I was burned out on the whole industry after nearly 18 years of writing and creating financial marketing plans and point of sale.

I wrote freelance financial newspaper columns for nearly ten years and kept a few consulting jobs writing annual reports and ad copy to keep the bills paid, but I still had my dreams of owning a creative business that more fit my talents and abilities.

Starting a Victorian Gift Gallery

My second husband is largely responsible for me being able to start a business. He encouraged me from day one and has been supportive all the way. He has unselfishly shared my time (which is little), supported me emotionally and financially and has reinforced my belief in myself when things are tough. I am fortunate to have him…he is a wonderful partner in life. As I have illustrated, timing is important.

My point is…most everyone will be negative, opinionated and unsupportive of your dream. The key here is to have desire, strong will and a burning passion to do whatever it takes to succeed. You are entering a marriage here…you will be tied to your business and it will consume you. You must put your total focus and energy into succeeding. Even when you do all this, you will still struggle, especially the first few years. Also, you will need a sizable nest egg to live on during your start up phase unless you have a supportive life partner. I am telling you this because it is not easy and you will not get rich quick. At this point, you are probably wondering why I am being so blunt. You must totally believe in yourself and that your idea will work! It is simple…If you can read all of this and still want to proceed, you have what it takes to succeed.

The birth of my retail store started one evening when my husband came home and wanted to go to the annual home show at the fair grounds. I had been writing all day and was not dressed to go out, it was very hot and I was in sportswear. He said, "Come on. You look fine." So we went. As I turned the corner of one isle, there it was, a booth of English and Victorian furniture with an authentic Englishman running it. My immediate reaction was of excitement. I thought…this is my kind of thing! We struck up a conversation and I made the decision right then and there to go into business following his footprints. He was a wonderful man who brought containers over from England monthly. I remind you, I had little money and a lot of dreams.

Over the next weeks I looked for spaces to put a storefront because he said he would work with me if I would purchase $10,000 of furniture from him. It may as well have been $100 at that time but I was hopeful. My husband and I agreed to put $15,000 into my new business venture, so I was in business.

I made the decision to open a 1,000 square foot furniture and gift gallery in Marysville, Ohio on the main street of town. My mother lived there and I wanted to work with her. My display window was unsurpassed. We truly stopped traffic. We were unique, had no competition and had a great business. We covered our bills the first month in business. This momentum lasted for two years, then the uptown revitalized causing street closings and lost parking spaces, which were at a premium in the first place. A large mall opened twenty minutes away and virtually every gift shop in the area started copying our gift lines. We dropped $2,000 in monthly cash flow.

Another rental space opened next door and we rented the extra space to have more exposure to the street traffic of over 15,000 vehicles per day. We thought this would be an excellent marketing opportunity to combine the two spaces. We had to remodel a small vacant building in the back of the present facility and cut two doors in the walls. The city inspectors had a big problem with this project, but we got it passed. Even with this new expansion, parking was a continual problem for our customers and the police officers were running people away issuing parking tickets. Some towns remove parking meters to help people, but this town didn't care if they ruined uptown businesses. Three uptown specialty shops opened and closed with three years.

Time for plan B. I had wanted to take the Victorian and English theme to the next step so I started planning a tea room. I had looked for a Victorian house for quite a while. I wanted to stay on the main street for higher exposure, so location was first and foremost. I found a Victorian house built in 1899, which was on the Ohio Registry of Historic Places. The property had the added bonus of being on a double corner lot on the highest traffic street of town. Although renovation would be needed, I still felt the house and double lots would be a sound investment.

We made an offer that was accepted, the bank approved our loan and the rest is history. We opened the tea room and gift gallery in 2000 with a bang. We were very popular and have maintained a good following. The recent recession and the economy have slowed our progressed, but we continue to thrive. Because we are in a fast growth county we are very optimistic about the future.

I knew from my past business experience that starting an entirely new business that I had never experienced would be difficult. I did a lot of research before I began. I felt that if I were going to operate a tea room, I certainly would want the best loose leaf teas available in the world. We are still using my original choice after three years of operation.

<u>Never underestimate county inspectors</u>. Now begins the horrid task of dealing with building inspectors, permits, licenses and local bureaucracy. Don't ever under estimate the egos and attempts of local bureaucrats to destroy your business and double your cost of renovation. I managed the renovation project, working with my son and the local **"gods"** who were over building inspections. I truly believe they were determined to stop a woman from starting a business in Marysville, Ohio.

The inspectors would not honor the building code for historic homes and enforced tough codes on our project. These protectors of the town tried to make us permanently seal the beautiful oak pocket doors in the house. They attempted to make us put an over 18 fire alarms and lights in the building that would increase our costs by 200 percent. It was as if they were there to destroy, not to build or remodel a beautiful old home. We appealed twice to the state board on key issues and beat the building inspector both times. Both appeals cost us weeks of delay on our project. Because of the delays we had already been forced to close our Victorian gift store uptown and had to put everything in storage. What a waste of money and time because of the building inspectors.

When it came time to put in the kitchen hood and install kitchen appliances and equipment I was ready for these great white inspectors. I hired the biggest restaurant hood company in the US to take these inspectors on and what a job they did. They made them look like fools because they were trying to enforce building codes that they didn't even understand themselves. How can a small business person win?

I tell you all these things because many people think of all the fun things about starting a business because they have no experience. Hopefully my background and experience will save other women a lot of heartache by helping them become better informed about all the issues or business "hats" one has to wear as you launch a new business.

My goal now is to teach and train others how to open and operate a tea room or any other new business one may wish to launch. There is so much to know and so many unknowns in the start up phase of any business. I hope to help others be successful and profitable more quickly than I have in the past ten plus years in business.

Tea Room Set Up

Depending on the tea room you are planning to open, the following will give you an idea of overall requirements and costs for a 42 seating capacity operation of 3,000 square feet. Each county will have its own guidelines and all inspectors will be happy to tell you what they are. Be prepared for a shock. This is where the unknowns appear such as our tea room size is 3,000 square feet yet the county required us to comply with the same rules as specified for a 12,000 square foot building. You will always need more money, it is never less.

·

For instance, in Union County, there were no codes for decks, and we had consulted Lowe's for a commercial deck blueprint and quote. Their design quote with an outline of materials needed totaled less than $6,000. We then asked the inspector to review the Lowe's plan thinking we were prepared to begin construction. What a shock when they literally destroyed the drawing. They required us to dig 42" footer holes (36 of them) instead of 36", use 6" by 6" wood columns (no code but they required it) instead of 4"x4" and numerous other changes in Lowe's plan. Our original quote of $6,000 ended up being $15,000 mainly due to their overkill. After labor was added the deck cost us $26,000. Much of the cost was due to extreme codes and requirements. Had we known this we could have added a whole addition to use year round. (Our first big mistake).

Then, there was the kitchen. What a nightmare. We had a new crew of engineers and inspectors in Union County so they really didn't understand most kitchen codes. They had to check a 12" thick book with every question. We hired American Ventilation, a 50 year old company, to install our exhaust system and they had to argue with the inspectors about several requirements. They could not believe what we were being required to do. My original quote for this was $4,500, which ended up being $8,500. We were livid, but without appealing, which we had done on two other occasions and won at the expense of two hundred dollars an appeal plus six weeks of delays, we simply complied. We were running out of patience, time and money.

Big egos are hard to deal with in this kind of situation, so investigate carefully before beginning your project. If at all possible, purchase a property that is grandfathered and has been approved and meets all codes for a restaurant. or **lease** (your start-up will be far less costly and more feasible if you do not have to incur a real estate purchase and renovations). Part of my business plan would include these issues before starting a project such as the one we started.

Dining Room

Planning the dining room is the most fun. You may choose your china, linens, silverware and décor. We were very frugal, doing most of the work within the family. We used a lot of creativity to enhance the ambiance. We were furnishing three and a half rooms and a 40 square deck for seating up to 80 people. All of the rooms opened to each other so colors and patterns were coordinated to be interchangeable. If your tea room is Victorian, follow a Victorian historical color chart. The details in this phase are very important because you never get a second chance to make a good first impression. When people walk in the door, they must feel welcome and be excited about the experience. Your décor and theme enables this to happen.

We frequented second hand shops, antique malls and watched the newspaper for good buys. We went to Dalton, Georgia to select our patterned Victorian carpeting, which saved us money and offered a quieter, richer environment. We chose a commercial dark leaf design that would not show soil. The burgundy, mauve and deep green color blended with the whole décor. Concurrently we painted and coordinated everything to be compatible. We faux painted the walls and kept patterns small so they would not compete with the merchandise we displayed. We researched our sources and shopped price to get the best buys. (When we enter into a consulting arrangement, we will share all of our vendors and suppliers).

It is important to determine each room's layout to capitalize on seating. A display piece of attractive furniture makes the dining rooms homey and welcoming, not to mention they afford an opportunity to merchandise appropriate inventory—both seasonal and year round.

When planning your rooms, keep in mind that many of your customers will be elderly or handicapped so leave room for wheel chairs and walkers. You will need an easily accessible handicapped rest room on the dining floor. This is a costly expense, but necessary and required to meet code. The list of requirements is overwhelming to the first-time entrepreneur; however, it is important to know what is needed to make an educated decision about proceeding with your plan to open a tea room.

Food and Menus

Creating your menu is where experience pays. Absolutely everything has a cost factor. From the very beginning, train your staff on the importance of controlling waste. Most of the foods served in a tea room must be prepared fresh daily. Scones and tea breads freeze well and improve in quality when baked right before serving. Soups can be held for two days when refrigerated properly. Salads and tea sandwich fillings should be made just before serving. Groceries will be about one-third of your overall budget. The secret to profitability in the restaurant business is cost management because it is easy to over buy, have too much waste and excessive labor. Be aware of these factors at all times. Profit margins in food service are limited.

Our business is fortunate because we have a Chef who shops daily for perishables such as vegetables and fruits. Our storage is limited so we are unable to order in bulk. We buy from a direct wholesaler and pick up staple items usually twice a week, more on heavy booking weeks. What is important is that you do whatever it takes to keep costs down, even if you must grocery shop yourself.

The presentation of your foods is extremely important. Garnish each plate with fresh fruit, vegetables, edible flowers and tea bread with flavored butter. We form tea sandwiches into numerous shapes, use different breads and change fillings each month to take advantage of the bounty of the season. Provide creative, colorful plates that look organized, colorful and appetizing. Never skimp on serving size or quality because repeat customers are the lifeblood of your business.

Pricing your menu is another area that requires in depth study. These costs can fluctuate because grocery prices go up and down in the marketplace. Stock up on sale items and order by the case whenever you can; however, this depends on your ability to freeze and store. Know what every item on the plate costs and allow for food cost fluctuations. Don't forget that labor and overhead plays a role in pricing. If you start out priced too low, it will be very difficult to raise prices later. Your customers will notice and get upset.

Note: When we are hired to consult, we offer you the option to purchase our popular recipes.

Staffing Can Be An Obstacle

Now I was ready to hire staff for the tea room. This was an interesting experience. I found that people who call themselves a chef are often trying to bluff their way into a higher paying job. I also found that some of them had huge egos and wanted total control of my kitchen even though they never put one dime into my business. Other's we hired tried to hijack me into higher wages or they would quit.

The people I interviewed had no knowledge of my experience hiring a lot of people and did not realize that I could quickly "see through" their façade. I had to hire and fire several so called "chefs" before ending up with an excellent staff. This is another area where I can help anyone in the restaurant business to hire the right people because I have an intuition and gift of finding the right people.

Budgeting

Your budget cannot be planned too carefully. Unexpected costs will always be a surprise as you tackle a remodeling project. There are two major parts to budget development. The first part is to develop your start-up costs. These are basically one-time costs you will pay as you establish your new business. Costs such as painting the outside of the building, remodeling, kitchen set up, handicap ramp and many other items go into your start-up budget.

The core of your business plan is called your operating budget. This is the budget you will live with month in and month out. This is the budget that shows a profit or the budget that will send you into business failure and bankruptcy. Your start-up budget and the operating budget must be developed by an experienced party or you will face serious consequences and surprise costs. Even with experience you will still face cost over-runs because you never see everything when starting a business. That is why you will want to develop a budget and then double almost all estimates, because your initial budget is only an estimate. Your real budget arrives after you have run your business for a while. I have helped many business owners save thousands of dollars by spending a lot of time getting solid numbers together to complete a business plan before starting a project.

Another major part of your start-up budget is called your break-even point. This is the point at which your business income is "breaking even" with your operating budget expenses. Many businesses fail because they never reach a break even point. You have to continually work on cutting costs and increasing income in order for your business to begin to break even on income and costs. The next step is to take your business to a profitable level so that you can draw your first salary as the business owner. No salary will be available to the owner until you reach the break-even point or your business will fail. This is called by some business owners as having the "staying power" to last during the start-up phase of a new business. The "staying power" usually will be referring to the first five years of the new business. These can be trying times if you don't have a sound business plan.

Marketing Your Business

Once you have completed your business plan, designed your business and completed your budget you will need to address how you will get customers into your establishment or expand your customer base, if you bought a current business. Many inexperienced people think that if they have a business people will flock to their door. That is a fatal mistake. With my vast public relations and marketing background, I still have to consistently work on marketing and business promotion. I have experience in doing press releases, feature articles, advertising, billboard advertising, newsletter publishing, mailers and flyers, buying mailing lists and numerous other marketing skills and I still have to stay on top of marketing my business. Until your business has sufficient traffic, you will never be able to stop marketing. This is one of my strong skills where I can be of tremendous help in launching a new business.

Business and Marketing Plan—Where to Begin

Your first step toward your dream of establishing your own business is to put everything in writing in the form of a business plan. Unless you have thought of every facet of your business operation such as location, start-up costs, operating costs and numerous other business issues, your dream will fail. This is a warning . . . anyone starting a new business that is of any sophistication who thinks they can avoid going through the detailed process of formalizing a written business plan will doom their business from the beginning.

If you have never done a business plan for a business and a marketing plan, that should be your first warning sign. If you have never done a plan for others or for your own business you cannot do your own plan without leaving openings for a number of huge financial mistakes.

Your second warning sign in establishing your business plan is that if you have never done a business plan for the specific business of your dreams you cannot do one without help. Trust me. I know because I hired a tea room book author and consultant and there were still some surprises. Without working with a mentor and consultant, you simply will not have all the components in your business plan required to make it successful.

I am reminded of a story about a young man who asked a rich man how he got so wealthy. The rich man responded, *"By getting experience".* Then the aspiring young man asked the rich man, *"How do you get experience?",* and to that the rich man said, *"By making mistakes!"* Making mistakes is a costly way to learn a business.

The young man's and rich man's story about sums up the average entrepreneur's way of gaining wealth. If you look at the wealthy people in America, they either inherited their wealth, own real estate or own a business. Few people ever become wealthy working for the other guy, but most people have no choice.

The moral of my own personal story and the value of this free report is to alert aspiring dreamers who desire their own business to the traps and solutions to starting your own business. To try a new business on your own when you have no experience is folly. To plan carefully, complete a business plan, seek out a mentor who will tell you the truth from experience and to do it with careful thought is the only way your dream will have a chance to become a reality. Without careful planning a dream can turn into a nightmare. The seven basic steps you should consider following when starting down the road to developing your own business are:

- Dream your dream
- Believe in your dream
- Act upon your dream
- Educate yourself in the business you are considering
- Complete a thorough business and marketing plan
- Begin implementing your business plan
- Persevere – you will need the "staying power" to allow your business time to grow

Mentor and Business Consultant

My 16 plus years as an executive in the corporate world and ten years of experience owning my own Victorian gift gallery and tea room, national business consulting, executive positions and years of public relations, marketing and communication gives me a tremendous ability to help women who want to try running a business. Whether you wish to run a tearoom, gift gallery or any other business, I can be a valuable mentor and business consultant. I feel I can save men and women a lot of money and even prevent some from making fatal mistakes. My warning to anyone considering launching a business is to do your planning with an experienced mentor unless you have a lot of money to waste getting experience the hard way. Trying a new business on your own is a formula for failure. There are simply too many "business hats" one must wear to be successful.

How I charge for consulting:

Business plan outline identifying all the components you must include in your business plan. This outline also includes your marketing plan outline. ***The consulting fee is $595 for a one-hour meeting and a final outline.***

- **Business plan completion - $5,000**
- **Hourly consulting – first hour is $350 and $150 there after.**

One year of on-site meetings for business launch, consulting regarding location, design, food planning, gift purchasing resources, web site development, implementing a marketing and public relations campaign, design of written material, open house and other requirements. My on-site one-year program is limited to 150 hours plus travel expenses. My fee for one year of on-site consulting is $30,000 ($ 10,000 initial retainer and the balance paid $10,000 at the end of the first quarter, $10,000 paid at the end of the third quarter. You will receive a consulting contract identifying the exact work to be performed based upon individual requirements.

You may meet for only one hour or negotiate how you would like to work with me. How you approach the idea of working with a mentor consultant is up to you. In a one-hour meeting I can quickly tell you if you should consider going further with your business idea. The time will be well worth the effort. I have invested a lot of pain-staking years to learn some of the things I have learned by trial and error and I simply will not give this valuable information away free. However, I will work with you in phases as you feel that is appropriate for your situation.

If you are currently in business or are considering starting a business you may wish to call me for a no-cost phone discussion. From our discussion you may feel I can be of help to you in your business interests. If so, you may contact me at:

Joyce Ann Whitaker
Owner

If you are long-distance, you may also call my husband at **The Advisor Group, Ltd. At (800) 800-5720.** Ask for Chuck. He is also a business consultant. Between the two of us, we can be of tremendous help to any one starting or expanding a business.

INTRODUCTION

ENGLISH TEA & VICTORIAN ERA GIFT SHOP

An English tea room and gift gallery conjures up instant memories of some of the family restaurants when you were a child where your parents took the time to talk with friends and socialize with people in the community. America has become so busy making money, owning things and leading a fast pace lifestyle that we have forgotten the old days when there was time to relax and have fun with friends, family and others.

We believe however, Americans are turning the corner. Just maybe we are getting tired of working all the time. Possibly we are beginning to understand the value of leisure activities and social visits with friends and family. We are realizing that our lives will soon be over and we are not really taking time to nurture relationships or stop to "smell the roses."

Social experiences are growing in popularity such as enjoying unique places that are elegant and quaint (tea rooms), visiting the beautiful treasurers of America such as Yosemite, Yellowstone, Grand Canyons, Mt. Rushmore and all other national landmarks. Maybe now is the time to enjoy the relaxed setting of a unique tea room of your own, one that represents the frills and fancies of the Victorian era for your own hometown.

WHY OPEN A TEA ROOM?

Operating a tea room is fun. The atmosphere is nostalgic, relaxed, friendly and elegant. You meet a wide variety of customers from all walks of life … professionals, businessmen and women, home-makers and retirees come time and time again, just for the simple pleasure of taking tea. The uniqueness of a tea room is your marketing edge because competition is extremely limited with most restaurants selling fast food that is pre-packaged and processed foods. Health consciousness is at the forefront of consumers with the baby boomer population desiring more than a trip to Wendy's, McDonalds and other fast food restaurants. The boomer's children are becoming teenagers and have their own friends. As these children grow up, the vast market of maturing boomers will seek a more relaxed, cultural environment as they transition toward retirement.

When you couple the boomers' lifestyle changes with the fact that tea is one of the fastest growing markets today, you will understand that the time is right to establish more and more tea rooms across America. In fact, many experts agree that the tea industry is where coffee was ten years ago. The health benefits of drinking tea supported by many national and international studies have awakened the consumer to the benefits of drinking tea. Those who establish a tea room, gift gallery and warm friendly dining experience in the next 10 years will have the opportunity to share in this once-in-a-lifetime tea drinking growth cycle.

JOIN THE TREND OF ENJOYING A CUP OF TEA WITH FRIENDS

Experts predict that the trend toward health consciousness and the need for a quiet, relaxed dining experience will far surpass the coffee drinking era before it is all said and done. The first step in developing the tea drinking trend is public education and that includes tea magazines. The industry already has several publications and tea associations that are setting the pace for public education and the promotion of tea. *The Tea & Coffee Trade Journal, Fresh Cup*, a tea magazine, *Tea Magazine* and the *Tea Room Guide & Digest* are helping set the trend.

Notes:

A BUSINESS OPPORTUNITY

THE GROWING INTEREST IN TEA

The desire to enjoy a more relaxed dining or social experience is prevalent among those recognizing that relaxing and enjoying life's experiences is most important.

Baby Boomers will set the trend simply because there are over seven times more boomers than there were in the "prime life" generation. Such a huge increase in the population will set new retail and social trends. Coupled with the fact that boomers are aging and their parents are living much longer, the reality of enjoying life in the present will become even more apparent. The boomers will likely become caregivers as they see their parents reach the point in life where they become totally dependent on others. Their own mortality will inspire them to enjoy life while their health is still good.

Another major change is the fact that the fast food industry has thrived on selling toys to children to build their fast food profits. The baby boomer children are growing up. They have their own friends and now the parents are seeking a better, more relaxing dining experience with friends. Tea room dining will help to fill this social need for a quiet, more elegant setting where food and tea are served.

Whether you realize it or not, the tea industry is about to boom in America. The engine is running and the race is about to begin. Fast food restaurants will be slow to catch the change to tea and now is the time to get into the business. If you have a good business plan, capital and have staying power to grow with the trend, join the race. As you know, the best money is always made with the number one and number two businesses that set the trends. How would you like to have started Kentucky Fried Chicken, McDonalds, Wendys, etc.? Don't you think an upper scale tea room and gift gallery would be a great opportunity? Well, we feel the "Cracker Barrel" style concept can easily work for a more sophisticated tea room.

THE HISTORY OF TEA

Tea drinking is almost as ancient as time itself. The health benefits of tea drinking have been known and promoted throughout China and Asia as far back as anyone can remember. From the time five thousand years ago when tea leaves from the Camellia Senenis tree fell into a pot of boiling water that Chinese Emporer Shen Nung was brewing until now, people have been drinking tea.

By 1650 the English had caught up with the Chinese, Indians and Japanese, etc. and were selling loose leaf teas from apothecaries for drinking enjoyment and for medicinal purposes. Prominent Englishmen touted the benefits of tea as a drink of choice.

"If you are cold, tea will warm you. If you are heated, tea will cool you. If you are depressed, tea will cheer you. If you are excited, tea will calm you." William Ewart Gladstone (1809-1898)

Thomas Garway, a merchant, was the first to sell tea at his Coffee House in Sweetings Rents by the Royal Exchange in 1658.

The tea business has come a long way with tea consumption growing year after year. Now with reports of the health benefits of drinking tea…its time has come. Couple a tea room with a nostalgic Victorian gift gallery and you can have a winning business opportunity…we are believers.

ASSESSING YOUR OWN BUSINESS EXPERIENCE

YOUR ATTITUDE

There are seven basic rules for being or becoming an entrepreneur and establishing your own business for the first time. Unless you have "staying power," you will need others to join you in your endeavor to open your own tea room business. Follow these seven rules if you are a want-to-be entrepreneur and you will go into your business with a much greater chance of succeeding:

1. **DREAM:** First, you must have a dream of your own.

2. **BELIEVE:** The next step to success is that you must believe in your dream one hundred percent.

3. **ACT:** If you believe in your own personal business dream, then you will begin to act upon that dream.

4. **EDUCATION:** Your next step is to educate yourself about your business by working in a similar business or reading all the books you can find or work with an experienced mentor.

5. **BUSINESS AND MARKETING PLAN:** You must develop your dream into a business and marketing plan. **<u>Your plan must be written</u>** or you can accelerate the process by following this business plan and hiring a consulting to tailor your personal ideas, budget and goals to your current situation. This would save you time and money rather than doing everything from scratch yourself. Seeking our help would not be useful unless you are **serious** about getting started in your own business.

6. **BUSINESS LAUNCH:** Once you have thoroughly evaluated all the pros and cons of your business and invested sufficient time to develop a sound business plan, you are ready to begin implementing your business plan. Your plan can be very modest or you can launch your business with a lot of capital; for example, locating your tea room in a new Victorian home in a high-priced neighborhood

with a 500,000 to 2,000,000 population. Whether you begin with a modest plan or launch a major construction project will depend on your experience, associates and available funding.

7.   **STAYING POWER:** When you start a business that is a good idea, is in the right location and has adequate funding, you must be willing to stick with it for the long term. Staying power is the key to building a successful business. You must allow a minimum of five to ten years to really build a truly successful tea room business. Getting a strong customer base takes time.

We still have people in our community of 25,000 population come in for lunch and say, "I didn't know you were here!" Yet, we currently draw patrons from throughout our state and across the country. After ten years of advertising, being on the front page of the local newspaper with full page articles, ads, promotions, newsletters, participating in community business promotions and all kinds of other promotions, some people still do not know we exist. In fact, we have over 15,000 cars go by our business daily and you can bet that these same people have driven past our business for ten years and still do not know what we are all about. Just remember, it will take time and you must never give up on a good idea. You will be able to build the customer base you desire slowly and surely.

WHAT IS YOUR WORK EXPERIENCE?

You will need to first list all of your work experiences in order to determine if you are a **good candidate** for setting up and running a tea room. If you have never set up a business or run a business, you will be in for a rude awakening of owning a business. <u>We believe that one of the best experiences in preparing for life would be to have every college graduate take a two-year internship in starting their own part-time business.</u> This would help them understand that business operations require a wide range of skills.

So, let's see what you have learned from experience in your career, job, social activities and community service that will help you as you determine whether you should set up your own tea room and gift gallery. This exercise will also help to identify the "weaknesses" in your experience so that you can find the right people to help you fill in the "gaps".

WHAT EXPERIENCE DO YOU HAVE?

YES	NO	YOUR LIST OF EXPERIENCES THAT MAY HELP YOU
❏	❏	I have run my own business
❏	❏	I have managed a business
❏	❏	I have done bookkeeping and accounting
❏	❏	My dad and/or mom owned a business
❏	❏	I hate my current job and have a strong drive to make a change
❏	❏	My back ground is marketing and/or promotion of products
❏	❏	I have a friend that will join me who has run a business
❏	❏	I have drive/leadership or have managed a community service
❏	❏	I never give up, am a self starter and have discipline
❏	❏	I have a business degree in marketing, finances or an MBA
❏	❏	I have a friend that is very successful in business
❏	❏	My health is great and I am energetic
❏	❏	I have a gift for interior design/color coordination
❏	❏	I love doing florals and my friends compliment my design
❏	❏	My food preparation skills are excellent and I enjoy cooking
❏	❏	I am very creative
❏	❏	I have leadership and can lead and manage other people
❏	❏	I am a decision maker
❏	❏	I know a lot of business people
❏	❏	I am a good writer and have worked as a professional writer
❏	❏	I can budget and manage money
❏	❏	I can work under stress
❏	❏	I can manage multiple tasks

This is only a partial for self-examination of your skills to determine what you can and cannot do because of your past experience or lack thereof. The more strengths you have checked and the more "yes answers" you have checked, the better your chances of succeeding!

THE *"BUSINESS HATS"* YOU MUST WEAR

Running a business is not easy and requires a lot of skill, experience and determination. To run a business you will need to wear the following "business hats" or have a partner or staff that can fill in for you. Even if you have a friend/partner or staff member that has leadership skills that you lack, you will still need strong leadership. The never give up attitude will help you survive the "ups and downs" your business will probably face. You will need creativity to come up with ideas to solve problems or your business will stagnate. You will need good people skills. You must have good business skills, be a hard worker and/or you will need to have a partner with strong leadership or the business will be doomed to fail. <u>Just being a nice person and having a financial nest egg will not drive a business toward success.</u>

BUSINESS "HATS"

_____

"Remember, if you haven't done it, you probably cannot do it alone"

YES	NO	WORK FUNCTIONS YOU CAN DO
❑	❑	Food preparation
❑	❑	Tea & beverage preparation
❑	❑	Inventory purchasing & control
❑	❑	Business management
❑	❑	Hiring & managing people
❑	❑	Developing new menus and food servings
❑	❑	Food purchasing, storage & management
❑	❑	Design & décor'/merchandising
❑	❑	Financing, credit cards, insurance & banking
❑	❑	Taxes & accounting
❑	❑	Legal issues
❑	❑	Marketing & promotion
❑	❑	Business signage & street image
❑	❑	Cost controls & management

FILLING IN THE "GAPS" IN YOUR SKILLS AND KNOWLEDGE

The first step in defining what you can do and what you will need from others to build a successful business is to <u>be brutally honest with yourself</u>. A warning sign that will tell you that you will need other skills is the fact that you have never run a business. If this is the case, you will be in for a rude awakening if you try to go it alone. With no experience in business, we suggest that you work for a similar business first, start a very small tea room or hire a tea room consultant to guide you the first year to minimize costly mistakes.

Once you have determined your strengths, you can now determine how you will handle areas of weakness. If you can't do accounting, bookkeeping and hate to cook, those are the functions you need to delegate. It is important that not all the skills you need to run a business will require hiring staff. For example, you can negotiate and pay a part time local bookkeeper to do your books, make payroll and other basic recordkeeping functions and then hire an accountant to do your tax forms and tax returns. By interviewing bookkeeping and accounting business owners in your area, you can easily delegate this work function. You can also develop a contact related to marketing and design of printed material, but be careful here. You can waste a lot of money in advertising and marketing that will not be effective. Carefully review the marketing section of this manual and learn from our experience and you will probably only need a small amount of design work and can carefully plan out a number of low-cost marketing techniques.

What about food preparation? Can you help out in the kitchen? Do you enjoy meeting people and being a host? Would you be a wise purchaser of the right inventory for your gift store? There are many other work functions that will be needed to run your tea room and gift gallery. Now take the time to identify the "hats" you may be able to wear if you are the owner of a tea room and gift gallery.

The above job functions and skills are what you will need to personally possess or recruit around you to run your business. This does not represent by any means all the skills required, but it will get you started on the process of self-evaluation to determine who you will need to help you run your business.

Once you have done a thorough self-analysis to determine the role you can play in running your business, you are now ready to determine the job functions you will need to complete your business plan. Now review the above list and write down the people skills you will need to compliment your own experience.

1. _____

2. _____

3. _____

4. _____

5. _____

6. _____

7. _____

8. _____

Comments and notes:

THE IMPORTANCE OF LOCATION

DEFINE YOUR CUSTOMER PROFILE

Tea room customers and Victorian gift buyers are not the typical "country" folks. The customer profile you are looking for when establishing a tea room is usually upper scale, upper middle class and retired women who have time and money to travel around to unique places. The market will change dramatically as the baby boomer realizes they can have a wonderful dining experience while purchasing a unique gift for a friend or family member and pay about the same price they would standing in line at a discount store.

You also will have many men that have learned how wonderful the food is in a tea room establishment. They find that they don't leave hungry, as many have thought. Our tea room patrons include judges, lawyers and numerous other professionals who have learned that our tea room offers more than the local restaurant down the block or the nearest fast food establishment. We are pleased to give ample servings and have a good reputation of always serving healthful, fresh foods, something the customer appreciates.

Because other tea rooms are springing up in our area, we are determined to be the best! Many, who have copied our menu and style, were open less than a year and closed. We attribute this to lack of knowledge and not realizing the work load and small profit margin of a start-up tea room. For goodness sake, be original and unique. Don't think you can copy another's success, unless you follow their guidelines to the letter through consultation.

HOW TO SURVEY YOUR MARKET LOCATION

The primary location for a tea room and gift gallery is in an upper scale business and residential area. Another key factor for location is street traffic. The more street traffic you have the better; however, you will need to check the city zoning and signage regulations because the size of your sign will have a lot to do with getting people going by your facility to stop and come in. Another great way we found to drive traffic into your business is to have a large display window with lots of unique color and design that can be viewed from the street. Drive by traffic is an important consideration regarding location.

To start your business out right you will need to complete a market survey so that you define your market right from the beginning. Specific research concentrates on solving the problem of competition and customer buying potential. While most big companies hire a marketing firm to gather the market data for them, you can do your own research. How you do your research will be determined by your own marketing experience and the funds you have to pay others to do it for you.

There are several ways you can do low cost research to determine a reasonable location for your tea room and gift gallery. Your local Chamber of Commerce will provide demographics of household income, age and community growth. For a few hundred dollars you can purchase mailing lists or simply call a mailing list company and have them run a count of specific zip codes in your area at no cost to get started. Purchasing an affluent women's list is a great start by selecting the upper scale zip codes within a 25 mile radius of the area you are considering as a location. Your prospect list should sort by income ($60,000 family income), select women age 45 plus, own a home and be in a key zip code area where upper scale residence live.

Another good strategy is to go to the local newspapers and television advertisers and tell them you are considering starting a tea room and would need to advertise. Ask for their research data and market statistics and review it to evaluate a site location.

Also, don't forget to look in the yellow pages for tea rooms in your area. You need to know if you have competition in the area you are considering. Go to the library and check with the chamber of commerce regarding other tea rooms in the area. You may also have real estate friends who can help you with identifying a good location.

DETERMINING YOUR STORE LOCATION

The two major aspects in locating your business are: 1) deciding on the particular community; and 2) choosing a site within that community. In choosing a community, the population in general should be a minimum of 100,000 or more. Ideally you would want a population of at least 250,000 or more, but that is not always possible. You can set up tea rooms in small towns, but you will need to totally scale down your business to survive in a small town. Consult with us if you are considering a small town versus a larger population area for your tea room. We can tell you how to do it successfully. We can save you a lot of heartache and money because we made mistakes relating to population and size of the town. Locating your business in a small town near a larger metropolitan area can also work with the right kind of marketing plan.

Another key factor in location is the income data available in the area. Where there are a lot of upper scale jobs people will have more money to spend. Make sure you get the average family income data as you evaluate your location. Blue collar employees don't patronize tea rooms as often as white collar employees and a mostly blue collar area is not likely a good location. Social class, a function of income, education, culture, upbringing, and other factors, strongly influences customer tastes and spending habits. Look for areas with upper scale housing, disposable income, family communities, older age range, leisure and recreational activities. Also, watch to see where the upper scale retail businesses are building their stores. This will give some indication of where the big stores consider a good retail area.

In summary, factors to consider in deciding on your tea room and gift gallery location are: 1) accessibility to potential customers; 2) traffic activity – we have 15,000 vehicles go by daily; 3) side street activity; 4) Property and city taxes; 5) restrictive regulations and ordinances; 6) whether to lease, buy or build; 7) over all population of the area; 8) affordability of property in the area; 9) distance from your home; 10) staffing availability; 11) how anti-business are the building inspectors; 12) disability, fire and zoning regulations. Don't forget the three real estate rules for a business, location, location, location . . . with convenient parking.

PARKING REQUIREMENTS

Lack of parking can kill your business. An inconvenient parking location will also destroy business activity. People are very busy today and are always looking for convenience. Make sure you have ample parking for your facility.

A 40 seating capacity tea room will require two handicap spaces and around 20 parking spaces for customers.

Make sure to check the zoning codes in your site area. Almost every city of any size has commercial, industrial and residential zoning. A commercial zone may allow certain types of businesses while an industrial area will not usually allow a tea room and certainly would not likely be a good location for your site. Check your zoning codes first before doing market research for a location.

SETTING UP YOUR BUSINESS

CHOOSING A NAME

Your name is crucial to the success of the business. The name should have class and convey an upper scale image. Our business started with **"Victorian Galleries"** because it was a Victorian gift gallery and the name served us well as a gift shop. After six years in business we decided to purchase a 103 year old Victorian house one block down the street and converted a former dental office into a tea room and gift gallery. We then had to consider changing the name to fit a tea room image and the name, **"Victorian Painted Lady"** was born for the tea room. The Victorian word allowed us to carry over the former name and "Painted Lady" represents the name for a Victorian house that is "painted out."

The name you choose should convey culture, some historic flavor and class. To come up with a name simply begin writing down every name you can think of without making a judgment.

Next get on the internet and look up the following words on Yahoo or Google search engines: **1)** English stores; **2)** English tea rooms; **3)** tea rooms; **4)** Victorian era; **5)** English tea cups; **6)** Victorian tea rooms; **7)** English and Victorian hotels; and other such names to get a feel of the era and culture. Make a list of names you like and then list all the names you have come up with and begin showing them to friends and ask their opinions. Listen to their responses carefully to get a feel for a name that will be accepted and liked.

Once you have decided on a name, you will need to decide on the type of business entity you plan to operate so that you can see if it will clear the business name registration office of your state.

TYPE OF BUILDING

We started with a up town store front for our gift store because the uptown address had a lot of traffic and it had a good display window on the street. A display window would normally only work for a business close to the street traffic.

Since the Victorian house we now own is on the same street a few blocks away, we still have the same traffic, but we lost the big advantage of the display window. We wanted to keep the historic value of the home and have not modernized it with a display window and only use the small windows to place Tiffany lamps with colored shades lighted at night for some street exposure, but the house is not close enough to the street for good impact.

Now that you see a couple of the issues we faced during our transition into a tea room, let us discuss the type of building you may wish to consider.

BUILDING YOUR OWN BUILDING

Ideally, the best bet is to own your own property and build a Victorian house in the right location with four to six thousand square feet of space. This would allow you to avoid "fighting" with building inspectors to get the business ready to operate. By building your own building you can hire a restaurant architect to design the layout for convenience and utilization. This is probably your best option if you have the money or know a good friend or banker with money. The reason is that most of the start up headaches will be on the contractor. In our case, we served as the general contractor to cut costs, but it wasn't worth all the headaches and we knew nothing about building inspectors at the time. Now we know how destructive they are and how they love to show their power and throw their ego around while trying to destroy your dream. But many people do not have the capital to build the ideal tea room facility.

BUYING AN EXISTING RESTAURANT

Another good suggestion is to lease or purchase a restaurant that is for sale in the right location where you can build a facade on the front of the building with an English or Victorian theme such as a porch to create a tea room image and remodel the inside to create a tea room atmosphere. The big advantage of purchasing an existing restaurant is that it is already likely zoned for your tea room, the handicapped regulations have been met and local people know the property as a restaurant. These factors get you a step or two ahead of getting the business up and running. The disadvantage is that the cost of remodeling the facility may be expensive because you will need to create a beautiful tea room image. You will need to create an **"experience"** for guests to set your business apart from the traditional restaurants.

Unless the restaurant facility has a lot of room, you may need to get a permit to add on a gift gallery to compliment the tea room. Why is a gift gallery a good compliment to a tea room? Because making money in food services is highly competitive, retail helps to increase income. You also want to give your clients a place to come for an experience. You want them to spend time in your home or tea room and relax. You want them to tell their friends about what a nice place you have so the referrals will build, which will help market your business. In our area here in Ohio we have the Cracker Barrel restaurant chain which has a **"home cooking"** type of menu and a nice gift store as you enter the facility. It is always busy and is popular with the average American. The building & restaurant has no color, unique architectural design, class or upper scale appeal. Their market is the average American going out for a reasonably priced meal. We are suggesting this same concept can be implemented with a tea room and gift gallery that has the beauty, color scheme and elegance of a bygone era. In fact, our facility has tremendous appeal as you can see from reviewing some of our pictures. Even children drag their parents into the tea room because it is so beautiful, inviting and comfortable. It is almost like going to grandmother's house. That is why you would need to remodel a facility to create a warm, inviting and nostalgic experience when designing an English tea room.

RETAIL LOCATION

Another suggestion is to locate a good retail store or restaurant in an upper scale area that is in a high traffic established shopping area and renovate the facility. Be very careful with strip malls. There are so many new malls being built that an older mall can quickly decline and close. Malls are dangerous but a good mall and a good location can have excellent foot traffic to help build your business. The disadvantage of a busy mall or a new mall is that it is a high rent district. Do your homework carefully if you decide to choose a mall retail location. Our thoughts are that malls are not the best choices. A storefront in a resort area or historic district are best.

BUYING A HISTORIC HOME

Another choice is to buy a historic home such as Victorian or Colonial and turn it into a tea room and gift shop. The big disadvantages of converting a home into a tea room are: 1) zoning may not be possible; 2) the disability act law will be enforced such as handicapped bathrooms, entrance ramps and other issues; 3) fire and safety codes will be heavily enforced; 4) inspectors will tend to ignore the historic building codes and try to enforce standard building codes. So, as you can see, if you plan to convert a beautiful historic home into a nostalgic English tea room and Victorian gift gallery, make sure you have plenty of time, patience and money. Triple your cost estimates because you will be shocked at the way the inspectors enforce their codes. We know because we went through hell remodeling our facility.

PIGGY BACKING WITH A RETAIL STORE

Finally, another lower cost way to set up your tea room is to find a friend with a retail business that has extra room and would work a deal with you to "hitch a ride" with their business. Be careful with this idea but the right location, right relationship and the right kind of upper scale business could work well for both parties where room to expand is available. Your business could serve current customers, give them a place to relax while shopping and bring in new customers for retail shopping. This is probably the least likely option, depending on your contact with the right business owner.

RESORT LOCATIONS

If you can move or buy a condo and live in a resort town part of the year, locating a tea room in a resort town makes sense if the season is long enough. The advantage of a resort location is that you will have an upper scale customer that is looking for ideas to entertain themselves while on vacation. They are there to spend money on themselves and to have fun.

Resort areas make sense because as the baby boomer ages they will be spending more and more money on recreation and leisure. In fact, owning a business in a resort area could be very profitable because the price of property will continue to skyrocket as the boomer continues to migrate to resort recreational business areas. Our belief is that normal housing and high priced residential real estate will begin to flatten out and values will even begin to decline as the boomers (seven times more people) have bought their retirement homes and stop buying as much real estate. We calculate that by 2014 you will see a massive booming resort and recreational business and the beginning of a major decline in residential real estate sales. There is absolutely no way that seven times more boomers will not impact residential housing as they buy their final home and turn to retirement, recreation and leisure.

Moving to a year round resort or living there during the peak season and establishing a tea room makes a lot of sense. Equity in your resort property would probably grow three times faster than property in most small towns.

If this idea makes sense, you will need to do all the research we have discussed. You will need to visit with the Chamber of Commerce and evaluate the type of tourists visiting the area, the growth of the resort business, tea rooms in the area, seasonal periods, building availability and the general growth forecasts for the future.

To summarize, choices for your facility and building criteria, a typical profitable tea room has ranged from 2,000 to 6,000 square feet of total space. Affordability is the key issues, for determining size and content. When renting, you will need to negotiate the types of renovation the landlord will need to do and you will need to have a lease arrangement where the owner cannot cancel your contract and ruin your business and at the same time you will need an **out** (such as 30 day written notice) on an annual basis in case the location does not work out for you.

Have a friend in contracting or an experienced real estate agent help you review all the property issues and evaluate what will be needed for your tea room. Make sure the owner takes care of all major renovation issues and negotiate the price for remodeling and repairs. If you get a triple net lease, you are responsible for all maintenance and repairs. Your available capital will determine how to negotiate these issues as you finalize a lease agreement with a property owner. Do your homework carefully because you will have to live with your decision.

UTILITIES

Your utilities can be very expensive. You will want to carefully check the past gas and electricity bills and evaluate the cost of your utilities, such as electric, gas, garbage, grease dump, telephones, sewage, security and fire alarm systems. If you centralize the floor plan carefully and locate a well insulated property, you can keep your utility costs down measurably.

We have a phone in the kitchen so the Chef can help answer the phone and discuss bookings and menus. The other phone is at the cash register. Another phone could be in your office. We also have Tiffany lamps and other lighting to show off our gift displays. Use of lower watt energy saver bulbs can help to keep down the electric bill. Dumpster and garbage bills can be negotiated if there is more than one service in the area. Make sure the pick up time corresponds with the time you will have full containers so that you are not paying for "dumping air".

Turn your thermostats down after peak hours, turn ovens off when serving time is finished and always keep windows and doors insulated with the right weather stripping.

Conservation of energy and recycling is very important. We also feel that regular insect extermination is essential for all food service facilities. One bad experience can ruin the reputation of your tea room. We were served a cockroach in our salad in a nice restaurant years ago and we never went back and never forgot the horrible ordeal!

YOUR KITCHEN

The kitchen is a very important consideration. Since most tea rooms do not fry food, a large commercial hood is not so important, but in our area the building inspector made us put in a large commercial hood anyway even though we do not serve fried foods.

Your kitchen should be laid out for quick access and convenience for the chef to get at things quickly. When the chef is really busy convenience is a very important issue. We have a relatively small kitchen about the size of a two car garage, but the layout makes it very efficient. Also, our downstairs is only seven steps down from the kitchen area and we keep the freezer and other items stored in the basement just off the kitchen

STORAGE AREA

Another important space is your storage area. You will always need an area to put things out of the way until they are needed. When shipments come in, you will need to keep them out of sight or competitors will sneak a peak at your sources. You also will need to unpack and price the items.

In addition, you will have floral supplies, gift wrapping supplies, damaged goods, dry goods, take out supplies and numerous other things that need storing out of site. We suggest that you have at least 600 square feet that you keep for organizing your storage area.

IMPORTANT FACILITY LAYOUT CONSIDERATIONS

The layout of your tea room and gift shop is very important. You will need reasonably quick access to your tea, beverage, ice, glasses, cups, napkins and utensils in order to serve your guests with as little travel as possible. The kitchen should also be close to the dining area to minimize food service time. The convenience of the food and beverage area to customer service will save a lot of work.

The tea room dining should have both private and open dining areas. Some people come for the privacy and quietness of the dining experience. Try to arrange the floor plan so that you have both choices. Those who want privacy can call ahead and make their request and reservations known.

<u>We do not have a room that will hold more than 15 in a group and this was a mistake we made</u>. You need a large room for catering weddings, church groups, tea society ladies, groups of military wives, red hat society groups, birthdays, showers, retirement events and other group activities. We have had as many as 74 red hat society women in a group, but we gave them the entire home for the event along with the deck. <u>We are missing a lot of business by not having the large banquet room</u>. There are two major advantages

when having a large banquet room; **1)** group guests become a marketing tool for your business; and **2)** you get larger food sales to beef up your income.

Your kitchen should have plenty of room for preparing and storing food. When you have a large group for lunch or dinner you will need the room. A small kitchen can be a nightmare. There is a lot that goes on in the kitchen, especially when you prepare food fresh daily with no pre-package bulk foods.

THEME, ATMOSPHERE AND MENUS

The theme for your tea room can be as creative or traditional as you choose. In our situation, we chose to buy a Victorian home, decorate in an old-fashioned way and serve with lace, china and crystal using three-tiered stands. We want customers to enjoy the nostalgia of stepping back in time. Our customers tell us over and over, **"The Painted Lady makes me feel like I'm visiting grandma's house."** This is just what we intended. A great deal of planning and know how went into our theme, which has resulted in our success. We are unique and we will continue to adjust to our customers desires. Every time we change our monthly tea menu, ladies cannot wait to try the new selections; therefore they come time and time again. Don't be fooled though … it requires creativity, research, time, marketing communication and organization to pull off something new month after month.

You will need to create your own house specialties such as your families' traditional menus passed through generations. In our case, we feature My Lady's Chicken Salad and Herb Chicken Salad, Spinach Feta and Broccoli Cheddar Quiches and several homemade soups every day. Our salads and dressings vary and may change seasonally. We make our own soup stock, salad dressings and desserts. We buy nothing prepackaged. Where can you find this kind of food in today's fast paced, profit-driven market? It is possible to find great dining experiences that provide a unique experience in some communities, but it is getting harder and harder. Our goal is to provide a cultural dining experience combined with a healthy menu and elegant tea service.

The key to operating a successful tea room is creativity, service, quality food and attention to detail. For example, you never serve a salad without very fresh greens and a refrigerated plate. You never serve soup that is not hot. You never have dishes and glasses that are not sparkling clean. Failure to attend to details can build or hurt your business. Repeat customers and referrals are your most valued asset. In our market area, three new tea rooms opened in the past year attempting to follow our example, which was very upsetting to me. Competitors and customers had come to our tea room seeking to learn how to duplicate our business and certain ladies had thought how wonderful and fun it would be to open a tea room in their community, not realizing just what it really takes to be successful. Now, after one year in business all three tea rooms and gift shops are out of business. I am assuming they were not adequately prepared for hard work and long hours and failed to have the necessary capital and creativity it takes to build and stay on top of their business. Yes, running a tea room can be fun, but there is an art to it.

Preventing future failure of well intended attempts to start a tea room is what this business start-up guide is all about. Coupled with our consulting, and helping people tailor a plan to their local community, we feel we can be the best "friend" anyone can have when they start their own tea room and/or gift gallery. We feel our mistakes and successes will be invaluable to anyone starting their own business. We hope that our knowledge and experience will prevent others from failing in this unique business that is fraught with numerous business traps.

THE GIFT GALLERY

Your gift gallery is your showplace to impress guests. <u>We made the mistake of mixing gifts with the tea room and we have found that most people are uncomfortable shopping in an area where people are dining.</u> You can display some gifts and larger furniture items in the tea room area for décor, but it is recommended that you have your gift shop in the entrance of your facility along with the cash register near the door way. This gives people who have to wait for lunch or dinner a chance to relax and shop.

Your floor plan should allow for about one-third of the floor space being used for the cash register and gift gallery. The larger your building, tea room and gift gallery is the more impressive it will be and the more of an experience people will have. That is too a point. If you have a 7,000 – 10,000 square foot facility it may begin to look like a retail store, but it all depends on how you lay out your facility. Larger is better if you have the money to design and stock your facility with small and large rooms rather that a having a retail store look. The size of your gift gallery floor plan will depend on the building and funds available.

FLORAL DESIGN

Another good addition to your tea room is a floral design service. In our original gift gallery we had the floral design space where the customer could watch us do the florals. We found that many of the customers really enjoyed watching the design of their florals and it seemed to be a good marketing tool and added to the experience of purchasing their floral. However, in our Victorian house we placed the floral department in the basement because of lack of room up stairs. We feel this is not as good as having the floral station where the customer can watch you while they wait.

For a floral department you will need a work counter, storage rack for ribbons, a supply of flower pots, accessable racks for a good supply of florals, tools and mechanics.

GIFT WRAPPING SPACE

Another necessity for your gift gallery is a space for gift wrapping. We have found that special gift wrapping services with quality paper in rich colors and satiny ribbons are a good marketing opportunity. We use a gold label with a line drawing of our Victorian house that really makes the gift stand out in the eyes of the recipient. Remember, this gift is going to someone who has probably never been in your store. Another reason to offer this "value-added" service is that most stores do not offer free gift wrapping. Customers are impressed with the fact that you provide gift wrapping and the fact that you really make a gift stand out as special.

For gift wrapping you will need a supply of nice gift paper, box filler, tissue wrap to protect the gift, several different size gift boxes and decorator bags, supply of ribbons, scissors and labels.

We suggest that your gift wrapping and floral space be combined so that you only have one rack for ribbons and supplies. We suggest a minimum of 300 square feet for this department.

TEA ROOM LAYOUT

Your tea room should be designed to provide small private dining areas, and bigger rooms for groups. Our home has a wrap enclosed porch that lends itself to more private dining for two. We also have two rooms that have "pocket" doors that allow us to close off the rooms for small private groups of 10 – 15 people. Customers sometimes like to dine in a more quiet area and these separate rooms allow for this convenience that they normally can't find in the traditional restaurant.

Tables should be covered with beautiful tablecloths (never plastic) with adequate lace or crocheted toppers. We highly suggest glass to cover the full table tops to keep laundry bills down and protect fine linens. We sell every topper we use, which counts for additional revenue.

The spacing between the tables should be ample for people to walk comfortably in and out of the room. We use round tables for some areas and in the hall way and porch we use smaller square tables due to the width of the hall and porch. Just use common sense in arranging the floor space for a comfortable dining experience. Chairs should not have side rails and need to be extra wide to accommodate larger guests. Your chairs must also be strong or larger guests will weaken them.

TEA & BEVERAGE AREA

Your tea and beverage service is very important and it should be located close to the dining area so the host and staff can quickly access beverages, ice, glasses, cups, utensils, napkins, creamer, water and other essentials.

Your ice maker will also be in this location. You will need a wash area for hand rinsing and washing certain items such as your fine china tea cups and tea pots and the pots for making hot water and hot tea.

Notes:

EQUIPMENT

You will need to think about the convenience of your layout, the daily activities and what is required to get your work done, not to mention the management of your business. The following is an over-view of the basic equipment you will need to run your business.

OFFICE EQUIPMENT

Basic furnishings such as a desk, calculator, filing cabinets, phone and fax to place orders and provide privacy where you can lock up and protect your private administrative files is essential. Only trusted employees or family members will have access to this area. You will also want a computer connected to the Internet or have one at home where you can do research, find new sources for gifts or check out competition, which is an important part of your duties. And finally, you will need basic shelves for catalogs and office supplies.

KITCHEN & FOOD EQUIPMENT

Essential equipment for your kitchen must be carefully thought out. One of the problems we faced when setting up our kitchen was the fact that the county inspectors in our area enforced all the restaurant codes such as a commercial hood and other ridiculous requirements. The reason the large commercial hood requirement was ridiculous was that we did not intend to serve any fried foods, but we had to meet the fried food preparation codes anyway. The local inspectors will mostly be your enemy and seemingly try to destroy your dream, especially if you are a strong businesswoman. We suggest that you use local contractors who already deal with the inspectors. It can save a lot of time, money and grief.

Here is a list of basic kitchen equipment we use:
- Commercial Convection Oven
- Overhead Exhaust System
- Automatic Sprinkler
- Commercial Gas Stove and Oven

- Heavy Duty Fire Extinguishers (check with your fire department)
- Commercial Refrigerator
- Commercial Freezer
- Food Processor
- Hand Sink
- Chef's Knives
- Dishwashing Sink with Drain Board
- Food Washing Sink for Food Preparation
- Salad Refrigerated Prep Table
- Commercial Mixer
- Commercial Toaster
- 3-4 Prep Tables
- Hotel Pans
- Silverware – salad forks, dinner forks, tea spoons, soup spoons, dinner knives, steak knives
- Dinner Ware – Salad plates, dinner plates, soup cups/saucers/soup bowls, bread/butter plates, platters
- Tubs for bussing
- Proper Wiring & Lighting
- First Aid Kit with Burn Ointment
- 3 Baking Stands/Racks
- Commercial Microwave Oven
- Ice Tea Maker
- 3 Hot Tea Pots (42 cup size)
- 2 Soup Kettles
- Numerous Storage Shelves
- Baking Pans
- 24 Cookie Sheets
- Utensils
- Frying Pans (All sizes)
- 2 Crock Pots
- Towels/Dishcloths
- Mixing Bowls/Storage Containers
- Ladles/Scoops – small, medium & large

- Chaffing Dishes
- Plumbing – Drainage Systems required- check county codes
- Emergency Lighting to Code

GIFT GALLERY EQUIPMENT

The equipment you require will depend on the theme you use. If you plan on a Victorian theme or other historic theme, you will want some antique furniture for display that fits your theme. Your antique collection can be a few simple pieces all the way to large rooms with several large antique pieces that are laden with gifts and walls filled with beautiful art pieces that take your customers back to bygone years. How elegant or basic your theme is will depend on your start-up budget. For an elegant theme, you can use simple things like battenberg lace and lace window dressing coupled with a few pieces of art and small antique pieces to keep the cost down. Follow your business plan budget to make these decisions.

The following are some of the gift gallery furnishings we use to create an elegant shopping experience:

- Large antique credenza
- Chippendale Upholstered Dining Chairs
- Buffet
- Wall shelves
- Nostalgic Lighting and Lamps
- Tiffany lamps
- Antique corner display cabinets
- Antique buffet display cabinets

DINING ROOM EQUIPMENT

Your dining room should be your showplace. The gift gallery theme should be carried throughout each dining area with a different color scheme to add to the experience for your guests. You can vary greatly when designing each dining area to avoid boredom. We follow a certain color scheme in each space. Customers usually develop their favorite room and ask for it when calling for a reservation. Your theme should be inviting, enticing folks to stay a while, socialize and relax from the busy pace of life. We merchandise carefully to give customers things to look at while dining. Visual appeal is your greatest asset …and never allow a speck of dust to gather on those valuable shelves and display spaces.

With this concept in mind, here are many of the dining room accessories and equipment we use in our 40 guest seating facility:

- 40 – 60 sets of Tea Cups/Saucers (Mostly floral bone china made in England, which are constantly on order because we sell them daily.)
- 40 – 60 Fancy Dessert Plates
- 12 – 16 Three-Tiered Serving Stands with Plates
- 120 – 180 Cloth Napkins (never use paper)
- 3 - 10 90" Tablecloths
- 10 – 25 60" Tablecloths
- 20 – 40 Table Centerpieces (candles/rings, etc.)
- 20 – 40 Salts & Peppers
- 3 – 10 Large Round Tables
- 4 – 8 36" Square Tables
- 10 – 25 36" Round Tables
- Lace Rounds & Squares to Fit the Number of Tables Used
- Crystal Sugar Containers
- Crystal or English Bone China Cream Pictures
- Silver Storage Containers
- Two – Four Water Sinks
- Designer Menus
- Mahogany or antique reproduction chairs for tables
- Desk & Chair for Reservations
- Window Treatments to Add Elegance
- Cabinetry and Displays
- Emergency Exits/Signage
- Fire Alarms to Code
- Check Pads
- Cash Register (basic or computerized accounting)
- Calculators

- Supplies for Rinsing Glasses and Cups, etc.

- Credit Card System

- Check Out Counter

- To Go Boxes

- Tea Pots/Bone China with Tea Cozies

- 3 – 6 42 Cup Hot Pots

- Ice Machine

- Shelving

- Serving Trays

Keep in mind that this list of dining room equipment will vary greatly, depending on square feet of space you have in your facility.

BUYING USED EQUIPMENT

It makes sense to purchase some used equipment while other most often used items should be bought new. However, by shopping around you may be able to find a restaurant or other business liquidating company to find great values for scratch and dent items you need. You can buy almost any type of second-hand business equipment by taking the time to shop around in larger cities. Businesses for sale, liquidation or consolidating are excellent markets for used equipment.

Carefully read the Sunday classified ads in most large cities for used equipment. You can also check with suppliers of new equipment for information because they often have repossessed equipment. In most large cities you will also find used equipment vendors as well.

If your start-up capital is limited, leasing may be your option. The advantage of leasing is that you minimize the cash needed to get started. A big disadvantage is that you are taking on debt service and payments that may consume your monthly income long-term. Another disadvantage of leasing is that there is no equity in leased equipment and you reduce the assets that will show up on your balance sheet should you need to visit your friendly banker for expansion later. A financial statement showing assets is an essential part of any business financial statement.

Tax-wise, purchasing is more attractive over leasing because of the depreciation and tax credit incentives for business. Another big tax advantage is the Investment Tax Credit or tax bonus you may lose when you lease. Talk to your accountant regarding which method of acquiring equipment is best in your own tax situation. There are no iron clad rules regarding which option to use, leasing or purchasing. By the way, buying used equipment is also a tax deductible business expense.

Should you decide to purchase your equipment using a bank loan or credit line, keep the loan period as long as you can, just in case you run into slow income periods or face unexpected expenses as we did. You can always accelerate the payments and pay the loan down early, but having this extra cushion may be a wise decision. We got hit hard with the March 2000 stock market reversal, 911 World Trade Center attack and the continuing three year recession. The unexpected circumstances can cause unexpected costs you may never think about and too much debt service can "sink the ship."

Regarding saving money, in general, you probably will be better off to spend whatever is necessary to buy new or new-looking fixtures and equipment to give your tea room a fresh look. Because start-up costs are so high, you may wish to cut corners in areas where you can without impacting your unique appearance.

Another good source for gift store equipment and food storage may be to carefully review what the vendors offer when you are purchasing inventory from them. Some of them offer displays when you purchase a certain quantity of merchandise. Be sure and check on this option when preparing to design your décor and ambiance. They may also have close-out items at excellent prices. Discounts can range up to 50 percent.

SOURCES FOR SUPPLIES & INVENTORY

It would be impossible for us to name all the worldwide sources for equipment and merchandise because new companies are coming into the market all the time, and you will want to make it your business to watch for the announcements of these new opportunities. You can do this by subscribing to trade magazines that cater to your business. The fastest way to check out these resources is to go on the Internet and do a search using a search engine. In the index of this manual we will list the categories and sources of where we purchase our food, inventory and equipment. If we are hired to do consulting we will research your area and provide a list of vendors.

CASH REGISTER, SALES TICKETS, MEAL TICKETS AND GROUP INVOICING

Your start-up budget will also determine how you will handle sales, accounting and tracking inventory. Your cash register can cost as little as $150 up to $3000 depending on what you want it to do. Whereas, a more sophisticated computerized cash register system may include total cash management, run all your financial reports, track inventory and give you a year end accounting for tax purposes. It will also do your payroll, track payroll taxes and retail taxes as well as provide you daily records. What you buy will be directly related to what you can afford. The advantage of a more sophisticated computer accounting and inventory system is that most of the bookkeeping and accounting and tracking is done automatically as you make sales. The big disadvantage of a larger computerized system is that you will need to be trained on the software and it will take time to learn the program in order to extract the benefits from the more advanced system. A small tea room running a weekly income of $2,000 to $4,000 may not want the more intensive accounting system, whereas, a larger facility earning $4,500 to $10,000 or more weekly may need better accounting, tracking and financial records.

FOOD PREPARATION

YOUR INITIAL SHOPPING LIST

This is based entirely on your menu. The correct procedure is to list every ingredient in your recipes including all staple items that are used in every kitchen, flour, sugar, salt, pepper, herbs and seasonings. Buy your staple items in bulk when you will be preparing the same recipes each day.

A simple start-up shopping list:

Salt

Pepper

Flour

Sugars-brown, cane & confectioners

Soda

Baking Powder

Yeast

Spices

Herbs

Vegetables

Bulk Canned Goods

Fruits

Cake Mixes

Pie Crusts

Meats-Chicken, beef, pork, luncheon

Cheeses

Pastas

Puddings

BUYING YOUR FOOD SUPPLIES

My chef and I shop daily for the freshest fruits, vegetables and meats. Bulk supplies are bought from a wholesaler that gives us a rebate at the beginning of each year. Our food costs run about one-third of the income.

TIMING, PREPARING AND SERVING FOOD

Creating your menu is where experience really pays. Absolutely everything has a cost factor. From the very beginning, train your staff on the importance of controlling waste. Most of the foods served in a tea room must be prepared daily. Scones and tea breads freeze well and improve in quality when baked right before serving. Groceries will be about one-third of your overall tea room budget. The secret to profitability in a restaurant business is cost management because it is easy to over-buy, have too much waste and have excessive labor. Be aware of these factors at all times. Profit margins in food service are limited.

Our business is fortunate because we have a Chef who shops daily for perishables such as vegetables and fruits. Our storage is limited so we are unable to order in bulk. We buy from a direct wholesaler and pick up staple items usually twice a week, more on heavy booking weeks. What is important is that you do whatever it takes to keep costs down, even if you must grocery shop yourself.

YOUR MENU & PRICING

Pricing your menu is another area that requires indepth study. These costs can fluctuate because grocery prices go up and down in the marketplace. Stock up on sale items that will keep and order by the case whenever you can use the supply up with little waste. This will depend upon your ability to freeze and store excess supply. Know what every item on the plate costs and allow for food cost fluctuation. Don't forget that labor and overhead plays a role in pricing. If you start out priced too low, it may be difficult to raise your prices later. On the other hand, if you start out with seemingly high prices, your customers may not become repeat customers or may come less often. Pricing will depend on local competition to some extent, but more on the sophistication and culture level of your target market. Affluent areas will allow you to raise your prices. Finding the right balance for your prices is an individual decision based on your costs and the market you serve. You may review samples of our past and present menus at the end of this section.

Another problem we have seen and heard from our customers is that many tea rooms provide such dainty servings of food that the customer leaves hungry. In fact, one well known tea room in our state goes to the extreme. Some of our customers have left this particular tea room and stopped by McDonalds to finish their meal. Finding the right balance for your service, food and quantity will largely depend upon your clientele. Men usually will require a more robust serving while elderly retirees may require a more modest plate of food.

The following are basic menu suggestions:

- Egg Salad
- Chicken Salads
- Green Salads-Homemade Dressings
- Quiche (varieties such as Spinach Feta , Broccoli Cheese, Bacon, Loraine)
- Soups-Homemade from hearty stock
- Hot Daily Specials
- Daily Dessert Buffet
- Scones
- Tea Breads
- Spreads
- Curds
- Devonshire Cream
- Seasonal Foods

STORING FOOD

There are strict codes regarding food storage and dating. Check with you local health department on this subject. You will need to buy commercial equipment, which can be costly. Always buy a larger capacity appliance than you need because you will grow quickly and won't need to upgrade. Also, a freezer is invaluable for food storage. Work out your procedures for dating food and train staff. Again, your health department will guide you on this.

PREPARING MEALS

Every morning our chef is in before 8 a.m. She makes fresh soup of the day, all salads and a hot special of the day. She bakes quiches every other day. Tea breads and scones are baked daily. We open at 11 a.m. and serve till 3 p.m. She has an assistant to help on busy days. Our staff helps as needed.

FOOD PRESENTATION

The presentation of your foods is extremely important. Garnish each plate with fresh fruit, vegetables or edible flowers and tea bread with flavored butter. We form tea sandwiches into numerous shapes, use different breads and change fillings each month to take advantage of the bounty of the season. Present creative, colorful plates that look organized and attractive. Never skimp on serving size or quality because repeat customers are the lifeblood of your business. Creating balanced menus with lots of fresh fruits and vegetables is essential.

SERVING *"HIGH TEA"* AND "PROPER TEA"

Many get confused about the terms of proper tea and high tea, when the differences are quite simple. A proper or afternoon tea is a light meal of finger sandwiches and mini desserts served with hot or iced tea. These are usually served on three-tiered stands at a coffee table or luncheon table. A high tea is considered a light supper with a main course (often a meat dish) on a higher dining table. This is always served after 4 p.m. If you add a glass of champagne or fine wine, the fare becomes a "royal" tea. All teas can become "themed" to celebrate the season or a special occasion.

PREPARING AND SERVING TEA

Each and every day we suggest you feature a "tea of the day." This will help to educate your customers and introduce them to new flavors. Of course, you will brew customer requests on the spot, but you will save time and money if there is a steaming pot brewed at all times. When you offer a sample of your daily brew it encourages customers to try new teas. Once they taste they usually say, "This is delicious, we would like a pot." There will also be customers who will drink nothing but Earl Gray or English Breakfast, which you will be happy to oblige. Sugar cubes, fresh sliced lemon or orange, honey and milk should be available at all times. We serve these accompaniments on decorative, hand-painted or crystal (small) plates or in dainty pitchers.

Remember . . . never bring your water to the boiling point. Hot water temperature should be between 180 – 185 degrees. Do not over brew or the tea will taste stewed or bitter. Most teas brew in 3 – 7 minutes depending on the type. Always preheat the service tea pot with hot water before pouring in the tea. Empty the first pot of water and refill, then add one teaspoon of tea per cup and one for the pot. Replace the lid, then cover with a tea cozy. Let steep for three to five minutes, more if you like a strong brew. Time depends on the tea and the desired strength. Serve in clean bone china teacups preferably from England. The English produce beautiful teapots and teacups that will last twice as long as others in the market. Cheap cups and pots do not hold up with daily service. Never present your tea service in stained or chipped or cracked teacups or teapots.

We started out with eight tea selections: Earl Gray, regular and decaf, English Breakfast, Victorian Rose (our own house blend), Jasmine (green), Oolong, Black Dragon along with Orange Spice and Raspberry. The mix was designed to offer black, green, fruit and herb teas. We now have 20 teas from which to choose and there are hundreds more available. We suggest beginning with eight choices and expanding as you go so that you can be consistently creating new teas to bring customers back. There are also seasonal favorites such as peppermint and orange spice in the fall and winter and Victorian Rose, apricot, peach and raspberry in the spring and summer. Iced tea is most popular when the outside temperature is over 75 degrees (you will need an ice machine). Some tea drinkers will have a hot tea even when it is 100 degrees!

Continually educate your customers of the health benefits of drinking tea, which contains flavenoids that strengthen and aid the immune system. Train customers on the different blends and their medicinal qualities such as peppermint, which is excellent hot for upset stomach or digestive ailments, sore throat, while cammomile eases stress and calms the nerves. Lavender soothes the soul and relaxes. Tea bathes are popular, so merchandise different tea products with their overall benefit.

The preparation of iced tea is just as important as hot! It should be crystal clear, never cloudy or muddy, which means you brew the tea frequently. The tea should be brewed just a little strong due to the melting of the ice. The perfect blend takes practice. Some teas are better iced than others.

When placing the teacup and saucer on the table, always turn the tea cup handle to the right at the right of the plate above the knife. Your server will always pour the first cup and place it in the proper position. Refill the pot as often as needed for the customer. You want your customers to drink the teas at their peak flavor and perfect temperature.

KEEPING YOUR BUSINESS FOCUS

WHAT DOES THE TERM *"FOCUS"* MEAN

Focus means the theme or image you desire for your business. Do you want a Victorian era feel, an antique or historic image, a modern image or a country image. We chose the Victorian and English image because of the house we purchased. We will never have modern or country gifts or have décor that does not fit that image. You do not want to mix images otherwise your customer will be somewhat confused regarding what your business is all about. Regarding a country image, we feel it is really difficult to portray a true English tea room image with a country crafts décor, unless it is sophisticated country. It is difficult to set yourself apart from all the country shops you see around small towns and it is certainly difficult to create an upper scale environment with the cheaper look of country crafts.

No matter what image you select as your theme, stick with it and do not mix a style, era or look. This helps you sell your uniqueness more readily. Stay focused on your theme.

THE HISTORY OF THE VICTORIAN ERA

Victoriana began in the mid 1800s when British Queen Victoria was born. She set the trends of the time with her style and grace. Every activity had a proper way of doing things. Fine linens, lace, china and atmosphere were the mainstay. When she married Prince Albert, the couple entertained in grand style using elegant settings and decorations. They enjoyed afternoon tea served on ornate silver trays and chose China tea service manufactured in Staffordshire, England. Elegant tea sandwiches and tiny desserts were customary menus served on library or tea tables. Once the British popularized tea time, it became a national tradition.

THE ENGLISH AND THE CULTURE OF TEA

Although the English copied tea drinking from the Chinese, the pomp and circumstance of the occasion is definitely English. The British culture would not allow for the no-handled teacups popular among the oriental people. They added floral patterns, gold and silver trims and the bone china composition along with the handles on the teacups and teapots. They also added the dainties that accompany tea drinking. No bare tables for the queen either. The more elaborate the tea fare, the more prestige the hosts gained. Everything was about appearance and finery.

THE APPROPRIATE DÉCOR' OF A TEA ROOM

If I were to describe the perfect tea room setting it would be pristine in appearance with soft, warm, welcoming colors rich in the heritage of the space occupied. Some research may reveal the perfect color scheme for your location. Peel wallpaper to the bottom layer or look under chipped or worn paint to discover what history has left behind. You can also research paint stores for the colors of the period the structure was built. In my opinion, nostalgic settings are the most refined for the tea room. You want visitors to feel welcome, somewhat like they are visiting your home. If you like roses then present them in abundance in your establishment. Lace, flowers, linen and crystal compliment the china and silver service you will be using to serve your guests. Always keep tables sparkling clean and linens fresh.

DISCOUNTING

After you have put a lot of time into designing a middle to upper scale image to attract the more sophisticated customers, why cheapen your image by discounting. If your décor' says, "This is a classy place" and then you try to compete with the discount stores, you are defeating the purpose of your image and focus. You will end up with merchandise that does not sell for one reason or another. In an attempt to sell slow moving merchandise, rather than discount it initially, try to move it around, put ribbons on it or add the item to a gift basket in order to make the sale. Be creative to keep slow merchandise moving. Don't establish yourself as a business where prices are negotiable or your will cut your profits immensely and begin attracting lower paying customers. You will begin attracting bargain hunters.

If you do end up with merchandise that will not move, then and only then do you have a sale maybe once a year by making it an annual clearance sale to make room for Spring merchandise. Just be careful how you word and promote your sale so that you don't appear to be a discounter. Have a legitimate reason for the sale that makes seasonal sense.

MAKING THE CUSTOMER'S VISIT AN EXPERIENCE

Every single customer that enters your establishment should feel welcome, be greeted with a big smile and be treated special. In a society that is fast-paced with lousy service, you can really make your business stand out in the crowd. There is not a single person alive that does not enjoy being catered to or made to feel special.

Some techniques for making a customer feel special and for taking your business to the forefront are listed here:

- Warm welcome upon entering the front door
- Ask if they would like to be seated or care to shop first
- Discuss private or open seating
- Hostess promptly seats guests
- Server is trained to welcome guests
- Server is trained to promptly ask guests their drink preference
- Dining tables and area are kept immaculate and dirty tables are never allowed in the area where seating new guests
- Ask for special requests
- Determine if occasion is a birthday or celebration
- Provides service until the guest has left and not leave guests sitting near the end of their visit

A simple candle in a dessert can make a world of difference in a birthday just as a word of congratulations can mean a warm response. These are the very actions that will bring your customers back and will inspire them to refer their friends, associates and family. Always strive to make your customers happy. Often you will get someone who cannot be pleased, but your reaction must be to **"kill them with kindness,"** which usually wears them down. However, never let anyone abuse your staff or cheat you out of your money. There will be attempts to damage merchandise to get the price down, but don't let this happen. Simply say that you do not sell blemished merchandise. We had a man tear the paper on the back of an art print to get a discount, but we saw him do it and it didn't work. Women have put pen marks on merchandise and ask us to mark down the price. In these situations we were courteous but firm.

FOOD PRICING

DETERMING YOUR COSTS

Determining your costs is the most difficult and important function you will perform. This is done carefully and precisely. Waste is the number one cause of loosing money. The amount of food you prepare daily is based on the reservations you have and the number of seats you have available. Account for every ingredient, prep time, overhead and profit. Be careful to investigate the competition in your area. You can charge more because of the elegance and experience you provide, plus you are serving made-from-scratch foods, which are healthy and have no preservatives.

Allow for prices to go up on certain seasonal items. If you garnish with fresh fruit, use seasonal fruits such as strawberries in June, grapes and apples in fall, melons that are on sale and peaches when they are harvested in late summer. You can vary selections based on current prices. Buy fresh items daily so they will not spoil.

In our opinion, lunch prices should be kept under $10 and teas around $13-$18. We provide our menu for some suggestions. If you have a best seller, be sure to keep the price consistent. Start out with a profitable price so you won't have to raise it later.

ADDING *"VALUE"* TO YOUR PRESENTATION

You can add value to your presentation simply by making the plates attractive. Of course, the quality of the food is extremely important. It is hard to find really fresh, "good" food in restaurants today without paying a lot of money, therefore, pay a lot of attention to every plate served. Slice the fruit in special ways, make sure it is cold and fresh, be sure the teabread is moist and not dried out. Scoop the chicken salad into a large mound and place on fresh leaf lettuce. Garnish the quiches with vegetables or fruit and specialty bread. If you serve a hot special, use casserole dishes or napkins and place on a larger platter with a side salad and bread.

Never serve old luncheon meats or cheeses. If in question…throw anything away that you would not want to eat yourself.

PRICING TEA & BEVERAGES

Pricing your teas and beverages correctly is essential because this is where you make the most profit. A teaspoon of tea costs around seven cents and you charge $1.50 per cup or $2.95 per pot. Some gourmet teas are more, but you really don't have to adjust the price because the most popular teas are the cheapest to buy. Tea tasting parties or twilight teas for a special promotion can help you sell bulk tea that is packaged attractively. **When selling bulk teas, remind your customers that one cup of loose tea at $3.50 makes 22 cups of hot tea.** Always provide directions for brewing tea.

PRICING YOUR "HIGH TEA" AND "PROPER TEA MENU

When you promote a tea of the month, you are taking the opportunity to raise your prices to introduce new menu items. These require special preparation so they simply cost more. The proper tea served daily at $12.95 can be exchanged for the special tea of the month for $16.95, etc. We celebrate holidays and seasons with special teas such as the Rose Garden Tea in June, the Pumpkin Patch Tea or the Bounty of the Season at Thanksgiving or the Victorian Christmas Tea in December. The going price for teas is somewhere between $12 to $20 with most upper scale hotels charging from $20 to $35.

PRICING GOURMET DINNERS

If you plan to serve gourmet dinners, you are talking a whole new ball game. You will need additional staff and much more money to buy food. Dinners stand to increase revenue, but it will take time to be successful. We have presented old-fashioned, comfort foods made from scratch – very unique in the market place. Plan a limited menu of comfort foods prepared by a chef such as filet mignon and portabella mushrooms, herb roasted chicken, sage-rubbed pork tenderloin and broiled lemon butter encrusted halibut. Offer sides of baked white or sweet potato, rice or pastas. A special salad with beautiful garnishes and homemade dressing is a real crowd pleaser when served very cold and fresh. Add home baked bread or rolls and you have a meal that is priced from $14.95 to $24.95. Desserts are priced from $4.00 to $5.50 and homemade soup of the day is $3.50. Don't even think of lower prices because you will not be profitable if the most you can serve is 30-40 guests at each turn of the tables.

PRICING LUNCH, CARRY-OUT AND DELIVERY MENUS

You charge the same price as on your regular menu! The food is the same and you have the added expense of carry out containers and special preparation. You can cut back on the garnishes if your patrons want only sandwiches and reduce the chicken salad plate to $4.95 for just the sandwich. You can offer free delivery if you have the staff to spare. Most orders are for pick up. Again, prices should range from $6.95-$8.95

PRICING SPECIAL EVENTS

A special event is prepared for in addition to your other daily food service. You usually price according to the number of people needing to be served. We always charge for delivery, set up and staffing when catered and when in house we add for extra service for large parties. If you are providing for decorations or linens and table service, be sure to get quotes from other suppliers. Provide a written contract and request one-half up front and the remainder one week before the event takes place with no refunds! Stick to this policy or you will experience slow pays and no pay customers.

Special events such as employee dinners, parties, retirement celebrations, birthday parties, corporate executive meetings, mothers and fathers day, church groups, Red Hat Society meetings, Tea Society groups and other such activities offers guests an excellent opportunity to market your business and can generate substantial income.

MERCHANDISING, DÉCOR & PRICING

GIFT GALLERY INVENTORY

Your inventory selection may be modest to launch your business; however, you will want to maximize your displays to add much needed profits. The way you arrange displays will help you promote quality and uniqueness and provide your visitors with an experience that will bring them back time and time again. Your displays will communicate the type of image you desire and set the stage for your reputation. You should stay away from **"modern"** display cabinets and opt for tradition furniture that you can sell. Expensive display units designed for mass merchandising can convey the image that you are no different than Wall-Mart or other commercial stores. Never forget that in order to compete with the big retail stores you must be different and provide a quiet service driven shopping experience the customer can't find at mass retailers.

Your inventory can be small, but convey quality with a reasonable price. You do not have to compete with large retailers, but unless your inventory is unique, there will be less reason to purchase from you.

Inventory turnover is another factor you need to consider. Turnover represents the number of times per year your inventory investment revolves or sells. Inventory turnover creates Gross Sales and the Cost of Goods Sold will be determined from gross sales. You will need to set aside funds to replace inventory as you make sales. The more you can turn over your inventory, the more your inventory dollars are working for you to make a profit. Customarily, larger items turn over very slowly, thus tying up your capital longer. The adverse is true for small items. As a rule, you will find new release merchandise placed in the right location in your gift gallery will have the highest turn over. Managing your merchandise purchases with these rules in mind will help prevent over-stocking, purchasing merchandise that doesn't move and avoid tying up your money in slow moving items.

The quantity of your purchases is another consideration. We tend to test an item with only one or two or a small number to try out new merchandise. On the other hand, hot items can be purchased with more quantity in your inventory. Another thing we have learned is that hot items will cycle and lose their demand – sometimes very quickly. Keeping your eye on trends and getting in early is the key to keeping up with good merchandise.

For the purposes of this business plan, we will give you three ranges of inventory quantity which includes suggested items for each category:

1.   **Small Inventory: $25,000**

- Tiffany Lamps
- Lace and Linens
- Teacups and Teapots
- Teas
- Stationery and Notes
- Cookbooks
- Greeting Cards
- Picture Frames
- Small Prints
- Dolls

2.   **Medium Inventory: $75,000**

- All of the items in No. 1 plus;
- Florals
- Throws and Quilts
- Artwork/Prints
- Crystal
- Home Decor

3.   **Large Inventory: $200,000**

- All of the items in No. 1 & 2 plus;
- Furniture prints
- Large Prints
- Bone China Tea Sets
- Silver and Brass

- Large number of antique furniture pieces
- Large number of reproduction furniture pieces
- Chandeliers
- Antiques

SELECTING YOUR INVENTORY AND SUPPLIES

Your inventory selection will be based upon the space you have available for your gift gallery. The size of your space will also help to determine the size and quantity of display units you need to present your inventory in a unique manner. We use a number of large antique and reproduction pieces on large walls and in the corners. We suggest this approach if you want to keep a nostalgic and historic image for your gift gallery. Your best source for display furniture is resale shops, yard sales, antique stores, estate sales and auctions. Nice used, antique or reproduction pieces are available for hundreds of dollars where modern displays cost thousands. For accent display pieces you may use glass upright display stands or small reproduction shelving as needed. We also keep our small jewelry and other items that can be stolen in a commercial glass display cabinet near the cash register.

Simply use your judgment based upon the kind of image you wish to portray. If you are in a country community, your image will not be looked at with as many critical eyes as you would experience in a more wealthy upper scale metropolitan area. Just be sure your appearance is well above the quality level of other shops and retail stores in your area so that you have eye appeal to impress your guests. People enjoy and appreciate quality and originality when they see it and a pleasant visit to your establishment will play a key role in bringing them back. If you impress people with a unique experience they will bring their family and friends to visit you to show off their new found place to go.

RESOURCES FOR PURCHASING INVENTORY

There are thousands of choices for purchasing inventory. We even visit estate sales and flea markets for special items that have quality and eye appeal. One thing we have learned is that mixing small and large antique items with new specialty items that stand out adds dimension and uniqueness to your displays. If you have the skill to spot value in used items, you will do well using this theme.

For new purchases, we have found that you will need to go outside of your local wholesale area so that you can find inventory that is different from other retailers in your area. We have a large wholesale distribution center near our location in Central Ohio and are able to find certain wholesalers that carry a unique line of merchandise and we do purchase from these quality local companies, but a lot of our inventory is from places such as New York, Atlanta, Chicago, Dallas, Seattle, England, Canada and California. By keeping your eye on the total wholesale market you can pick up very marketable and unique gift items for your gallery. Manufacturers, distributors, import sources, national trade shows and visiting sales reps are all sources for locating merchandise.

Another rule we have is that your average gift lines should be under $25. Large items take time to move and your money will be tied up longer. Too many large items will prevent you from keeping a fresh look in your store.

Here are some companies where we purchase our inventory:
- Meyda Tiffany & Paul Shalin Tiffany
- Quality British Imports
- Peking Handicrafts
- Upper Deck
- Pacific Rim
- JB Lamp Supply
- Showstoppers and Delton Dolls
- Schilling
- Bouquet Enterprises

To find other sources you may get on the internet and use a search engine to locate merchandise by putting in words such as wholesale gifts, international wholesale gifts, wholesale gift baskets, display cabinets or furniture, etc. You may use categories also such as lamps, clothing, crystal, etc. Use your creativity to locate a number of wholesale resources. One word of warning is to be careful that your provider carries quality merchandise. The sources we have listed are ones we have found to provide quality and reasonable prices for the merchandise they offer.

MANAGING YOUR DISPLAYS

Rotating displays on a weekly or bi-weekly basis is a good habit to get into. You will find that merchandising and changing a display will boost sales. What might not sell in one location will sell in another room or location.

SUPPLIER FINANCING

Wholesale suppliers will not normally finance your inventory with 30 day net until they work with you for a while. Some will work with you after the first order while others never finance a very small business order. You will want to check with each supplier to determine how they work with new businesses. Sometimes when we need something quickly and it is a small order, we just have it sent COD and pay upon delivery.

Your bank is not likely to finance inventory unless you have a strong financial statement. However, if you have a piece of real estate, it is usually easy with reasonable credit to finance your inventory with a second mortgage. As a word of warning, you do not want too much debt that will create big monthly payments or you could be jeopardizing your business. Only purchase the amount of initial start-up inventory you can afford and only buy ongoing merchandise as you can afford to maintain or expand your display lines. Start small and gain experience as you go. Acquiring a lot of credit with slow inventory turnover can bankrupt your business. Start out by working with your vendors and learning who will give you a 30 day billing and minimize the use of vendor credit unless you will have the money to pay for the merchandise. Never count on selling merchandise to pay your invoices unless you have a very good customer base to create regular cash flow.

DESIGN YOUR COLOR THEMES

One of the tricks to successful merchandising is to use color to define a display. This is so easy and effective. Group like colors and textures to improve your display to enhance the visual appeal and demonstrate how the items will look in the home. This also masks the fact that you may only have one or three of a kind in the collection. Vary heights by using boxes or cans and cover them with beautiful coordinating fabric in an artful manner. Use floral arrangements to pull the colors together and add a romantic flair to the display. Always be aware of the season and add at least one focal display to celebrate the current holiday. Common sense dictates your color usage. If you have a pink room, try to feature colors that look good in the room such as sage green, aqua and other shades of pink from dark to light. Remember the rule of working in odd numbers 1, 3, 5, etc. unless you are using a pair of lamps or vases, etc. on a mantle or buffet.

SOURCES FOR STORE DISPLAYS

Your first choice is to find good large pieces of wood furniture to accent your gift store area. Your next purchases can be smaller wood tables, stands, corner cabinets and shelves that will fill in the smaller nooks and crannies. Another option is to talk with your vendors to see if purchasing a certain amount of merchandise will give you free display opportunities. For example, we have a line of teas that come in quality wooden boxes and displays that allow us to present our teas in a way that is very inexpensive. These displays are used over and over again and cost us nothing.

Other sources for display merchandise are local antique stores, used business furniture and restaurant equipment stores. In our area, we have several used stores that offer some display items we can use and still maintain our unique image. Again, check the yellow pages or go to the library to locate alternative choices in your area. Discount hotel furniture outlets are also a good source for quality and unique display pieces because most of the inventory is top of the line with wood carving and fine woods. You can paint, stain or sand to achieve the look you want.

COMPUTER INVENTORY TRACKING

The problem we have found as a small boutique business is that we have been too busy to set up and learn to operate a more sophisticated computer tracking system. That does not mean tracking inventory manually and visually is the way to do it, but we have not had the time or the staff to computerize our inventory. We run our business daily and keep our eyes on inventory using our experience and intuition. We do not carry a lot of any item except teas, cups and saucers, teapots, etc. and we keep a written log of sales and what is needed.

Absentee owners will definitely want to consider a good computer system for all income, expenses and inventory, otherwise it would be impossible as an absentee owner to really track the business. The system should also provide complete financial summaries, cost of goods sold, income statement, assets and liabilities, purchase orders and a balance sheet along with tax friendly annual reports so that you can easily do your business taxes at year end.

The extent that you computerize your business will depend on financing, time availability, size of the business, onsite or absentee ownership and many other factors. We recommend the accounting and business management be discussed with your CPA and speak with computer consultants in order to decide how you will set up your cash register, accounting, inventory tracking, tax record keeping and normal business records.

CALCULATING YOUR MARK-UP

Your mark-up, to some extent, will depend on your local area and a lot of other factors. Your image and location will also have a lot to do with price mark-up. If you have a low-budget image, customers will expect bargains. If you market to bargain hunters you will have less mark-up because customers will expect lower priced goods. On the other hand, if you present an unusually upper scale appearance, have more expensive looking wood display furniture and demonstrate quality, your price can be higher.

Mark-up and gross profit on a single item is often confused because a product margin when expressed as a percentage is always figured as a percent of the selling price while mark-up is usually figured as a percent of the wholesale or seller's cost. For the purposes of this discussion on mark-up the formula to determine your retail mark-up would be cost plus operating expenses plus desired profit margin equals the total mark-up price for a retail item. Unless you make enough money on your inventory to replace your cost-of-goods-sold and pay your overhead each month you will never be able to take a salary from your business. However, if you price your merchandise too high for your customer base, you will be known as a gift store or tea room that is really expensive. Pricing your merchandise is a judgment call on your part based on where you locate your store and how you establish your image. It is important to open your business with a feeling that your prices are fair and that you have quality merchandise. With that image you can afford to mark up your small to mid-sized merchandise from 100 percent to 200 percent. Sometimes a very small jewelry item can be marked up 200 percent of your cost price, if it is an unusual piece while a nationally advertised item may need to be reduced. The more you may offer one or two of a kind items that are not found locally, the more freedom you have to mark-up.

INSURANCE AND RISK MANAGEMENT

UMBRELLA LIABILITY INSURANCE

Going into business increases your liability for accidents on your property, lawsuits and product injuries. You will also be driving on the highway on behalf of your business and business assets could be exposed to a vehicle accident. These liabilities should be protected with umbrella liability insurance. In fact, every American should own this insurance, whether in business or an employee.

One form of liability insurance is an umbrella policy or an extended liability insurance that extends your home and automobile liability protection. This type of insurance "wraps" around your current insurance and raises the limits of protection should you be in a lawsuit that would go beyond current policy limits. Every American should carry $1,000,000 to $5,000,000 in extra liability insurance. Why? An example would be a situation where you caused a bad vehicle accident and you caused the death of two people and injured one other person. What do you think a lawsuit would claim as damages. Would your current vehicle insurance cover most lawsuits of this type? Not likely. Anyone who owns a business or has personal assets could lose these assets should a lawsuit exceed current insurance protection. For this reason all of us need to carry umbrella liability insurance. After all, the premium will only be from $200 to $500 annually.

In general, individual umbrella insurance covers the following risks:

- Homeowner's insurance – expands your personal liability, medical payments to others, property damage and bodily injury.
- Automobile insurance – expands your vehicle liability, medical payments and other injuries caused while driving or a passenger in an automobile.
- Watercraft liability insurance – expands liability due to injury or damages while in a watercraft.

In summary, this extended individual liability insurance provides a larger amount of protection than is available under other policies and helps to broaden your protection, filling in the gaps that may exist. Umbrella policies generally have fewer exclusions than other policies.

BUSINESS AND PROPERTY LIABILITY INSURANCE

Customers entering your property can have an accident walking on your stairs, trip and fall down and break a leg, get cut while looking at a gift and breaking a glass piece or some other freak accident that could lead to damages. You name it and some business somewhere has faced justified and ridiculous lawsuits from customers. A prime example is the lady that was trying to drive and drink hot McDonalds coffee. She was awarded millions in her lawsuit. She should not have placed the coffee in her lap in the first place, but McDonalds was considered liable by the courts.

In general, the following risks may be covered by insurance:
- Loss of property damages such as buildings, fixtures, supplies, merchandise and business assets.
- Loss of income resulting from interruption of your business caused by damage to company operating assets.
- Personal injury to employees and the general public.
- Loss to the business caused by the death or disability of key employees or the owner.

FIRE INSURANCE

A standard fire insurance policy pays only for fire related losses. Other losses such as:
- Continued expenses (after a fire) such as salaries, rent paid in advance for a temporary facility while your property is being rebuilt and other obligations should also be covered by obtaining business interruption insurance.

WORKERS COMPENSATION INSURANCE

- Workers' compensation laws also require that you provide state sponsored or private compensation insurance that protects you from employee injury liability while on the job. Such issues as safety negligence, faulty equipment and other working conditions can cause liability and protection is necessary to protect the business from such potential risks.

You can purchase insurance to cover almost any type of risk. The following types of coverage are most commonly used by business owners:

- Fire and general property insurance for fire, vandalism, hail and wind damage.

- Plate-glass insurance covering window breakage.

- Burglary insurance for forced entry.

- Fidelity bonding – covering theft by employees.

- Consequential loss insurance – protecting your business against special losses due to fire damage and business closure.

- Fraud insurance – to protect the business against bad checks, counterfeit money and larceny.

- Public liability insurance – covering injury to the public while on your property.

- Product liability insurance – to protect from injury to customers arising from faulty products and goods.

- Workers' compensation insurance – covers injury to employees while on the job.

- Life insurance – covering you against loss due to a key employee's death.

- Business interruption insurance to pay for loss due to business closure and other losses in business activity.

To purchase insurance you would normally talk with a casualty agent who provides a variety of business insurances. Make sure you work with an agent that represents a number of companies and one that has several years experience working with businesses.

PERSONNEL AND HIRING

STAFFING REQUIREMENTS

When we started our business we had only two part-time staff members. As the business grew over the years we slowly added part-time and full-time staff. As owners, we have worked long hours to manage the business and to keep labor costs as low as possible. You have to sell a lot of food and gifts to pay for one new person.

We found that hiring a chef was a real challenge. Most people claiming to be a chef who responded to our ads were a fraud. They really were not a chef but wanted $25,000 to $40,000 in pay. A small tea room and gift gallery cannot afford to pay this kind of wages.

Our menus were developed by us and we totally manage the kitchen, so why did we need a chef? After all, the chefs we attempted to work with were awful. They wanted to take control of our kitchen, didn't understand our focus, didn't know what they were doing, wanted helpers so they did not have to work or wanted to hi-jack us for more money. We found a better way to deal with this problem.

When we purchased the 100 year old Victorian house and converted it into a tea room, we wanted a chef, but finally ended up with the owners doing the cooking to develop the menus. Then we began training one of our staff to cook and prepare the food. This experience has taught us that a tea room does not need a chef, but what it really needs is a good employee who enjoys preparing food and one that is teachable. We found that when we hired a so-called chef, they already thought they knew it all.

Your kitchen help is a major key to your business. The next most important employee requirement is a friendly server that will make the customer feel welcome and provide efficient table service. Again, the best people we have are those we have trained from scratch. A desire to learn and a good attitude are more important than past experience so long as the owners have the capability of training. In our case, we came from the corporate world and have managed people for years. We feel we can motivate, compliment and recognize the work of good employees and turn them into great employees.

In summary, for a small tea room and gift gallery we have found the best and most loyal employees have come from recruiting novices who need to work, have a desire to learn and have an attitude of service. Our employees have come from women who have had little or no experience but really wanted out of their situation desiring something to do. That desire, coupled with compliments, training, supervision, strong policy and constructive criticism and recognition has caused these women to blossom and grow into friendly, warm and loyal employees.

The following is a list of employees we have for our tea room and gift gallery along with their basic job descriptions:

- **Head cook and kitchen manager** – The skills desired are creativity, culinary experience, cleanliness, organized, good with people, management skills, can work under stress and can handle numerous responsibilities.

  Responsibilities – Cook daily (lunch & tea) menus and help in the preparation of gourmet dinners and for special promotions such as grill outs. Create new menus and attractive presentation, prepare special orders of customers such as menu dishes, decorated cakes, etc. Manage the service flow and staff of food preparation. Oversee the ordering and stocking of food and supplies to be purchased for the kitchen's operations. See that the kitchen is kept clean and assist with that duty. Work with owners to improve operations, making suggestions as needed in areas that could be enhanced. Oversee the requirements of the Health Department and informing owners when issues need addressed.

  See that quality, cleanliness, freshness and presentation of food is always at its best. Assist with any kitchen or service task that is vital to the efficiency of customer services and daily operations.

  Inform owners of any problems or potential problems before they escalate. Let owners know if there is time available or a desire to help with the retail or serving side of the business.

- **Management and Kitchen Manager Assistant** – Responsible, dependable, ability to work with people, can work under pressure, can carry out the direction of management and handle numerous and varied responsibilities.

Responsibilities – Assist Kitchen Coordinator with all kitchen assignments as needed. Assist with daily (lunch & tea) menus and help in the preparation of gourmet dinners and for special promotions such as grill outs. Help with the service flow of food preparation. See that the kitchen is kept clean and assist with that duty. Wash dishes, help bus the dirty dishes on busy days and assist with any task that improves efficiency and timeliness.

Work with owners to improve operations, making suggestions as needed in areas that could be enhanced. Assist with retail sales and service when called upon by the owners and act as owners back up as directed when they are away. See that quality, cleanliness, freshness and presentation of food is always at its best. Inform owners of any problem or potential problems before they escalate. Let owners know if there is time available or a desire to help with the retail or serving side of the business.

- **Server/dining room assistant/dining room cashier** – Dependable, honest, good customer relations, can work under pressure, can carry out the directions of management and handle numerous and varied tasks, accurate and strong attention to details. Must be assertive with troublesome customers and not allow them to push staff around or try to get a discount.

Responsibilities – Prepare and set tables for lunch and dinner activities. Take orders and serve food. Act as expeditor for keeping food service timely and efficient. Assist dining room manager with assignments as directed such as water, coffee or tea preparation.

See that beverage and soup service areas are kept clean and stocked. Wash dishes in beverage or kitchen area as needed, when kitchen staff member(s) is absent or when time is available. Take turns carrying dirty dishes to the kitchen staff if they are busy and need help. Dust, sweep or perform cleaning and organizing as requested. See that quality, cleanliness and presentation of food is always at its best. Assist with any kitchen or service task (food service or retail) that is vital to the efficiency of the business operation. Assist with retail sales and customer relations as needed.

Inform owners of any problems or potential problems before they escalate and let owners know if there is time available or they desire to help with the kitchen side of the business.

The number of employees in each category will depend on the size of your business and whether you serve lunch and tea, dinners and a Sunday brunch. We currently have two full time staff and three part-time staff along with one owner working. We alternate the part-time staff based on whether we have a busy day or slow day. You will need to determine your staff based upon your own business goals. One thing we learned is not to hire experts! We find people who are teachable and in need with a good attitude. With coaching, love and recognition, they usually make great staff.

STAFF WAGES AND PAYROLL

- Head cook: $9.00 - $10.00 per hour + payroll costs
- Assistant manager: $6.00 - $7.00 per hour + payroll costs
- Servers & general help: $5.00 – 6.50 per hour + payroll and tips

WORKING AND BUSINESS HOURS

Our business is in a small community of less than 30,000 population with the largest metropolitan area of Ohio (Columbus) about 30 minutes away. We could have dinners and Sunday brunch, but we have chosen to keep our life simple and only open for lunch and tea from 11:00 am to 3:00 pm six days each week and the gift shop is open until 5 pm. If we were to expand our hours we would have Friday night and Saturday night dinners and Sunday brunch. We may still add dinners and brunch to our menu.

We suggest that a tea room and gift gallery in the right location with a larger population than we have would be wise to start out with lunches and immediately begin promoting special dinners, special events and Sunday brunch. Once you get customers used to your business hours, it will take more advertising and marketing to change or add new hours later. We feel that if you are going to offer dinners and brunch, the best time to begin promoting these services is with your initial launch, not that you can't do it later, but it will require re-educating your current customers.

TAXES, ACCOUNTING & LEGAL ISSUES

DECIDING YOUR LEGAL ENTITY

You have a number of choices for legal entities (state authorized legal names and types of business, i.e. corporation, family limited partnership, etc.) that you may consider. The following list and brief definitions of legal entities will provide you with an over-view of your choices:

- **DBA or Sole Proprietorship** – This is simply a state registration of a name and means, "Doing Business As." It may be your personal name or a fictitious name that will be cleared by the state you live in. The state corporation registration office will tell you if the name is taken or available. In Ohio we pay $50 to register a name with the state.

  We do not recommend using a DBA normally because your business liability will all be on you personally and all your personal assets will be exposed to the liability. This is a cheap way to go, but does not convey longevity or present a credible image to the public – certainly not like a corporation or limited liability company.

- **Family Limited Partnership (FLP)** – The FLP is a separate legal entity that may be used for a business. This type of entity has been around for decades and has a lot of court case history regarding its ability to protect business liability from personal assets. Sometimes a business owner will put his or her major personal assets in an FLP and make the business an "S" corporation to begin a new business. **This is an excellent way to start a business.** You will need to consult with your attorney regarding local state laws and get their advice on how best to structure your business. The parties controlling the FLP are called General Partners.

  Both the "S" Corporation and the FLP pass through the profits and losses to your personal 1040 tax return. This is done by a business accounting form called the K-1. This allows you to write off start-up business expenses against your personal family income to reduce your personal income taxes during the start-up phase of your business.

- **Limited Liability Company (LLC)** – Limited companies are relatively new in most states. In Ohio they were officially recognized in 1995. This entity was formed after a number of celebrated national lawsuits that caused national companies, including a big eight accounting to fail. Lawyers, politicians and CPAs decided it was time to separate the professional liabilities from personal assets and to separate member liabilities. Thus the LLC was born.

  We operate our tea room as an LLC. We suggest this form of entity if you will have partners in the business. We like this form of business entity for our business. No business liability will typically penetrate our personal assets. Also, to look at the downside of things, if your business fails it will not bankrupt you personally. Personal assets may be placed into a family limited partnership (FLP) and controlled by your family living trust.

- **"C" Corporation** – This is often referred to as a regular corporation. This type of business entity is most commonly used for successful companies that make a large profit. We would not suggest this form of corporation be used for a start-up business unless your attorney says otherwise. This corporation is taxed as its own tax entity with the IRS. If you have a lot of money and want to set up employee benefits, this type of company offers some good benefits opportunities.

Once you have selected a business entity, you will need to have your CPA complete an IRS form called the SS-4 form to file for a business tax ID number authorized by the IRS. See your CPA or go to the government web site at www.irs.com and get the form to request a tax ID number.

Make sure you understand the advantages and disadvantages of each type of business entity before making your final decision. Seek the advice of a business attorney and CPA before deciding what to do. However, we suggest that you never risk your personal assets when starting a new business. It is never wise to place years of savings and assets at risk with a new business. Seek the help of an advisor before you structure your business plan.

BUSINESS TAX OPPORTUNITIES

Owning your own business offers you the opportunity to write off most any business expense any large corporation has as a tax deduction. When you own a business you want to learn how to take business trips rather than vacations. You will want to write off your automobile as a business expense. You may need health insurance and other employee benefits and these are also mostly deductible.

If you have never run a business, you would be wise to go to the library and find two or three business tax books that tell you how to maximize the tax advantages of your business.

WORKING WITH BANKS

Business oriented bank loan officers will work with you if you have a good financial statement, fair to excellent financial and credit record and they will be happy to assist you in funding certain business needs. Our business banker has been terrific and has worked with us through some tough times during the recent recession and the 9/11 recent terrorist attack.

If you have a poor credit history and only a few assets, forget the banks. *In fact, you will need to acquire other financial partners to help you create your dream if you have poor credit and insufficient funds.* Also, if you flunked the experience checklist, you may be wise to forget starting your own business without good mentors or a business partner.

Talk to your friendly banker or look up SCORE, a retired business consulting group in your local area and meet with them to see if your ideas make sense. By visiting with your banker and SCORE, you will be able to get some idea if you are on the right track.

CONTROL YOUR BUSINESS START-UP DEBT

When we started our business almost eight years ago, we did not have nearly enough capital to begin a business. By the time we established a business name and business entity and purchased inventory we had a lot of money invested.

We found a really good banker who worked with us to finance certain parts of our business. Later on when we bought the Victorian house and remodeled it into a lovely gift gallery and tea room, we found the county building inspectors to be real "devils" because they acted as if they wanted to destroy our dream. We had to fight them, appeal and win and continue to challenge their interpretation of the county code. In many cases they were totally wrong in their interpretation. Our battle with these men with big egos almost sunk the ship. These unexpected financial challenges can cost a lot of money.

To get our tea room up and running, we experienced cost over-runs of thousands of dollars and we had to visit our friendly banker again. This time we had to take a second mortgage on our property to finish up the project and purchase nine rooms of furniture, furnishings and gifts. In all, the project ran over $90,000, much more than we had planned.

Be very careful you do not go into debt too much because the monthly payments can easily **"sink your ship".** Your business will take time to build and if your monthly payments exceed the income, you can get into trouble quickly.

FINANCIAL MANAGEMENT

The best way to manage your business finances is to purchase a business accounting package or hire a bookkeeper and work with a CPA. You will need to keep track of your fixed overhead, variable overhead, cost-of-goods sold and your purchase orders in order to keep your expenses in tune with your income.

The first phase of your business is called the **"start-up"** phase and you should consider this the first year. During the start-up phase you are marketing your business and developing income. Almost always, you will confront surprise expenses and learn of obstacles you will face in your business. When you plan your business always plan on contingency dollars that are set aside for these surprises. Without back-up funds the business could easily fail.

After one year, your ongoing operations should be pretty well figured out regarding income and expenses. Your goal and challenge will be to reach a business break-even point as soon as possible. Your break-even point will be when your income and expenses regularly break even. Some businesses take five years or longer to reach this point. That is why you must do your home work well in advance of jumping in. A strong marketing budget is the key to a fast business start.

Don't ever start your business if you have never owned a business without reviewing your finances with your banker, SCORE, CPA, attorney and a tea room consultant.

ACCEPTING CREDIT CARDS, CHECKS AND LAY-A-WAYS

Your business must accept credit cards and checks when you own a small business. In our eight years of business we have only had three checks bounce and we have collected all of these bounced checks. When you take a check, make sure to get a driver's license number, current address, current phone number and their Social Security number.

To set up your credit card system you will want to work with your local bank where you will deposit your checks and other income. You will typically pay a set up fee and a percent of credit card sales. Shop around in your area for the best deal so long as the bank is convenient for daily depositing of your income. Try to negotiate loans and do your business at the same bank so that you can build a strong banking relationship.

If you do take lay-a-ways you will want to set policy on how long you will hold the item and collect a non-refundable deposit to assure that the person will return for the item. We do allow lay-a-ways because most of our merchandise is one-of-a-kind and if a customer really likes the item but needs time to pay for it, we provide this "value-added" customer service. People who are serious about an item will appreciate your kindness and it will also bring them back to your business. They may even have the money for something else or have lunch upon their return.

PAYROLL RECORDS

Keeping good payroll records and payroll withholding taxes is critical to keeping abreast of costs. Taxes must be collected and employee benefits must be deducted (if any) when paying your help. A low cost bookkeeper or a organized system can help keep you on top of your payroll records.

If you are keeping things simple and using a one-write system, you will need to issue pay statements. If you use a computer system it can be set up with the payroll tax and benefits accounting to automatically issue statements and track all payroll. How you go about your payroll recordkeeping may vary based upon whether you use a bookkeeper, CPA, computer or other method of keeping records. Your state retail taxes (if applicable) and payroll tax withholdings should be set aside in a special tax savings account so that you have the funds to pay them when due. Failure to do so will probably get you into trouble with the tax department. There is nothing more certain than taxes and death. Owing taxes can encumber your personal assets in most cases.

Your payroll will determine your tax liability and withholding payment requirements. Seek advice from a bookkeeper, CPA and computer specialist before making your final decision on how you do your payroll. Your local ADP representative may be another choice to do your accounting and payroll.

Payroll records require 20 different kinds of employment records that must be maintained just to satisfy federal requirements. These recordkeeping requirements are:

Income Tax Withholding Records:
- Employee name, address and Social Security number
- Amount and date of each payment of compensation
- Amount of wages subject to withholding for each payment
- Amount of taxes withheld from each payment
- Reason the taxable amount is less than the total payment
- Statements relating to employee' nonresident alien status
- Market value and date of non-cash compensation
- Information about payments made under sick-pay plan
- Withholding exemption forms completed
- Agreements regarding the voluntary withholding of extra cash
- Dates and payments to employees for non-business services
- Statement of tips received by employees
- Requests for different computations of withholding taxes

Social Security (FICA) Tax Records:
- Amount of each payment subject to FICA tax
- Amount and date of FICA tax collected from each payment
- Explanation of the differences – if any

Federal Unemployment Tax (FUTA) Records:
- Total amount paid during calendar year
- Amount subject to unemployment tax
- Amount of contributions paid into the state unemployment fund
- Any other information requested on the unemployment tax return

Check with your CPA to make sure you are complying with these tax regulations.

BUSINESS LOCAL, STATE AND FEDERAL TAXES AND LICENSEES

No matter where you live in America, there is always some bureaucrat that will be there to collect taxes, licensee fees and charge you for permits. If you have never been in business you will be shocked at what the system will put you through to run a business. You will fully understand what bureaucracy is really all about. It is a miracle any new business survives by the time a small business plows through the paperwork, serves as retail sales tax collector, collects payroll taxes, does accounting, reporting and bureaucratic obstacles we all face to run a business. By the way, politicians don't even know what a small business is because they refer to a small business as a business with under five million dollars in income. That is why the truly small business never really gets any help to reduce the obstacles bureaucrats place on businesses.

You will need to talk to local business owners, tax advisors and/or business consultants to find out what you face in your local community. There are always business licenses, sign permits and approval procedures, zoning ordinances, remodeling permits, county permits, state licensing, federal licensing, disability act requirements and other local issues. You will be closely monitored by the health department and experience numerous inspections annually. You will need to learn about all these issues before starting your business. Often there are more rules to follow within the city limits than outside the city jurisdiction. Do your homework before starting a business.

You will also want to familiarize yourself with deceptive practices such as false advertising, misrepresentation and simulation of competitive products. You will want to avoid badmouthing competitors and keep up on violation issues of the manufacturer or distributor of products offered by vendors. A fairly common statute forbids the sale of any article at less than the seller's cost if the intent is to injure competitors.

TAXES

A business owner will be responsible to collect various state and federal taxes and remit them to the proper agencies. See your tax advisor to set up your tax records and tax collection system. The following taxes are part of the required withholding process:

- **Income Tax Withholding** – the amount withheld will depend on the employee W-4 form disclosing the number of exemptions each employee has listed on the form. The percentage is figured on a sliding basis and IRS tables are available for weekly, biweekly, semi-monthly and other payroll periods.

- **Social Security (FICA) Tax** – Federal law requires that the employer match the employee withholding tax. You will need to get the withholding chart or see your bookkeeper.

- **State Payroll Taxes** – Almost all states have payroll taxes of some kind. Unemployment taxes and state income taxes are two typical withholding taxes. Again, check with your CPA on your local tax laws.

- **Personal Income Taxes** – As a sole proprietor you will not have the employee tax withholding as employees do but you will be required to pay monthly or quarterly self-employment taxes. Your local IRS office or the web site can provide the 1040 ES forms to file. Again, see your tax advisor regarding what you are required to pay.

- **Corporate, Limited Partnership or Limited Liability Company Tax** – Normally these entities file an annual tax form at the end of the tax year, whether calendar or physical year.
- **Retail Sales Tax** – Sales taxes are levied by many cities and states.

- **City Taxes** – Many cities also charge a local tax or payroll tax. Talk to your tax advisor regarding what is required in your state.

USE OF ADVISORS AND CONSULTANTS

The extent you will need advisors and consultants will be determined by your own experience or the lack thereof. Advisors and consultants can help you identify the "holes" in your experience and identify the type of business team you need to succeed. For a small tea room and gift gallery you will need advisors that know the business; otherwise, they may steer you in the wrong direction. In past years during the late 70s we had a business that was growing rapidly. Our income began as a meager $95,000 and within three years we were generating over $100,000 monthly. The growth was so fast we could not find a business administrator or business manager that could work within the framework of an entrepreneurial growth business. Every administrator we found was accustomed to operating a well-oiled administrative system and we had none. Our business changed daily and our advisors were **"full of bunk"** because they had no entrepreneurial experience. It is very important to befriend a tea room and gift store owner and seek the advice of those who have the experience; otherwise you may be paying for worthless information.

Go out of town or even out of state if you have to in order to get experienced help and to build a valuable long-term relationship with other tea room consultants who are owners. <u>We went to a tea room owner in another state we knew and paid them a good consulting fee to get started</u>. We knew that with no restaurant or tea room experience it would save us money and reduce a lot of mistakes we would have made on our own.

We offer a two hour consultation in our tea room to assist those who have purchased our manual. We also offer to provide direct consulting in your community to assist in making the right decisions regarding location, building layout, avoiding problems and set up and décor of your facility. However you decide to get started, you will need direct help if you have never run a business or set up a tea room. If you have no real experience in the restaurant business, get help or you will wish you had later.

ADVERTISING, PROMOTION AND PUBLICITY

DEVELOPING YOUR PRINT IMAGE

Your printed image can convey success or failure. <u>You will never get a second chance to make a good first impression.</u> Your printed image should convey the image of your tea room and gift gallery. In our business we continually convey the Victorian and English image and stick with this theme in our newsletter, menu, brochure, advertising and other marketing activity.

We have a line drawing of our house that portrays its Victorian architecture, as you can see from the small picture at the top right on this page. The décor of our business conveys quality and the colors of the interior are inviting and friendly. You can use pictures of your own business to convey your theme in your printed image as well as use some clip art that fits the era you wish to portray.

Basic printing that will carry your image or theme may be developed by a designer or yourself (if you have experience) and the common images and pictures can serve multiple purposes as you develop other print projects. Brochures, business cards, flyers, menus, newsletters, a web site and other marketing media can all use the same image and artwork once it is completed and put on a disk. You may also want to go to a search engine such as Google or Yahoo and type in Victorian clip art, English clip art, Victorian pictures or other image you wish to portray and you will find a number of free and low-cost sources for clip art to compliment your image development. Be careful with free clip art because the "dot density" is not strong enough for quality printing.

YOUR MARKETING BUDGET

Unless you budget a reasonable amount of money for marketing your business may not get off the ground. There are low-cost techniques for marketing and there are expensive opportunities to market your business. The three most expensive marketing opportunities are television, magazine and newspaper advertising. Publicity during your grand opening and initial launch of your business will offer you the lowest cost marketing opportunity for media releases, newspaper articles and possibly TV coverage. We have taken advantage of all of these options.

We do not recommend that you spend less than $10,000 for your marketing start-up budget to get off the ground the first year. We will discuss several marketing options later in this section. On the other hand, if you are establishing a large tea room and gift gallery of five to six thousand square feet, we suggest that you invest up to $30,000 in the first year to market your business wisely using a number of the methods. A very small boutique tea room will need less and a very large facility will require more marketing to build a base of customers.

We are still shocked at the people who come in after eight years in our small city of Marysville, Ohio who say, "I didn't know you were here. I wish I had known about you!" This still occurs to this day in a city where we have run ads, set up exhibits during street festivals, had full page newspaper articles, grand opening pictures, had front page newspaper feature stories, sent newsletters, held open house events, promoted Victorian style shows, had a beautiful street side store display window, had signs on a main street where 15,000 cars a day go by daily and participated in numerous other events. Some people are simply not observant and you have to keep marketing to get their attention. It would be nice to simply invest in an initial marketing program and after that people would continue flocking to your business, but it does not happen that way.

Regarding your ongoing maintenance budget, depending on how well your are doing after the first year, you will want to invest from five percent to fifteen percent of income into marketing activity of some type to maintain and continue to grow your business until people are standing in line to be seated.

PRE-MARKETING YOUR BUSINESS

Once you have a rough idea when you will be able to open your business doors you will want to begin pre-marketing your business. There are a number of ways to do this. Here are some suggestions:

- Visit the Chamber of Commerce in your area and ask them for suggestions and they will probably help you get some free promotion – that is if they are alert.
- Prepare professional media releases and send releases to all newspapers, radio stations, local magazines and television stations. Include a picture of your self or your business with the release.

- Develop a newsletter announcing your opening, describe your services and mail to affluent women in the area. There are two list companies we use to buy list of names:

  CIS – 612 Corporate Way, Valley Cottage, NY 01989, (800) 547 – list,

  Fax: 845-268-7629/ Email: CIS@CISMarketing.com

  Web site: www.cismarketing.com

  American List – 88 Orchard Road, CN 529, Princeton, NJ 08543

  (800) 252-5478 (888) 830-5478 Ext. 3022 Fax: (908) 874-4433

  Email: list@amlist.com   Web site: www.amlist.com

  Names will normally cost you from $75.00 to $120.00 per thousand names. We have bought from 2000 to 13000 names for our mailing at various times.

- Another excellent pre-marketing approach is to simply design a nice six by ten card and mail it to your target market area (See enclosed examples).

- Finally, you can offer a fund-raising event for churches in the area and agree to donate five percent of all sales to a church or community social programs so long as the funds are paid directly to a qualified non-profit 501 (c) 3 organizations so that it is tax deductible. The funds may go to any church funding need such as a teen group function, senior activity, helping abused women, funding a children's cause and other community social needs.

PROMOTING YOUR GRAND OPENING

Holding a grand opening is an excellent opportunity to acquire free publicity. Your grand opening can be as simple as setting a date two to three weeks in advance of the event to having a larger scale event that can include a fashion show, music and entertainment or a local paid entertainer or local author present to help you maximize the potential for your event.

Certainly you will want to have the Chamber of Commerce officials come by for a newspaper and/or TV photo opportunity. Prizes, refreshments and drawings always offer additional opportunities to promote the event in the local media. Use your imagination. We have used musical entertainment such as a dixie land band, harpist and a guitarist player for special events entertaining. Keep the music and events in tune with your tea room theme. Tea and tea tasting are also great activities.

SEEKING FEATURE ARTICLES

Editors and the media **are not looking** for opportunities to promote your business for free. They **are looking for newsworthy events** that will be of interest to their readers, viewers and listeners. You will need to have something unique and newsworthy to get feature articles.

A few years ago we had the largest newspaper in the area send one of the **"Grumpy Gourmet"** restaurant critics to our tea room unannounced and never revealed that they were present. Later on a client told us about the article in the restaurant review section and how horrible it was about our establishment. When we read the article we could not believe what was being said about us. The article stated we charged $3.00 for a cup of coffee, that we served coffee in a Styrofoam cup, which we didn't even have in the tea room at that time. This was totally untrue and the entire article was false. We called the columnist and informed him of the mistake and he immediately retracted and offered a special front page story and picture of our Victorian tea room in the business section. Of course, we had threatened to have our attorney sue for damages.

Well, we used that as an opportunity to launch a feature article. We called the editor of the "Grumpy Gourmet" restaurant section of the paper and said, *"Grumpy Gourmet, this is grumpy Joyce and I will have my attorney contact you unless we can work something out to correct the reporting errors you published!"* The editor of the review of local restaurants agreed to make it up to us. After follow-up calls and hounding the editor they sent a photographer to our business and took some pictures. The photographer was specifically told to get a picture of "Grumpy Joyce!" Well, guess what. The picture and a large half-page article was placed on the front of the business section of our major Ohio newspaper. It pays to operate with strength rather than weakness and be persistent. The article is enclosed.

Other events may lend opportunities to get publicity. You just have to be creative. One of the most recent feature articles we had was a very successful event that developed from an organization in our county. A newly formed military family support group was organized by a local retired general. Our tea room was selected for the first social event and we served a patriotic luncheon complete with yellow rose corsages and flag centerpieces. We received a call from the organization wanting reservations for approximately 40 military wives. The more we thought about this the more we realized anything related to the war in Iraq offered a great feature story opportunity.

We got on the Internet and used a search engine to find all the local magazine, newspaper, TV and radio media contacts. We typed up a media release and called all the media to ask for their help in promoting the event. It only took about a day to gather the information, contact the media and complete the promotion of the event. We received excellent interest in the program and a front page story with a color photo appeared in the local newspaper. The military support organization loved our media promotion because they needed to raise money for some of the families who were having a tough time financially during the time their spouses' absence.

Always be looking for a newsworthy event you can promote through your business to get the media involved. Special events – whether planned or a natural part of your business – offer great opportunities to get your name in the local papers.

MEDIA RELEASES

Attached you will find an example of media releases that demonstrate exactly how you lay out and write a media release. It must be done in a formally accepted format or the editor will likely ignore your release.

- The key components of a media release are:
- An eye catching header
- Topic specific
- Total explanation in first paragraph
- Contact person/number
- Details
- Close

EVENTS MARKETING

Throughout the year there are events that provide your business with the opportunity to promote special occasions. Christmas is the biggest annual event to feature your business. Maybe you would like to sponsor a Christmas Tea for needy children. It can be a tremendous boost to your business. Your Christmas promotion should begin with a Christmas Open House just after Thanksgiving. The event should be promoted well in advance to allow customers the opportunity to set the time aside to attend. Plan to offer free tea and scones and tea bread.

There are many other special events around which you can plan promotions and special events such as:

- Mother's Day
- Father's Day
- Thanksgiving special
- Valentine Day
- Sweetest Day
- Secretary's Day
- Mother & Daughter etiquette dinner and class

We also promote a special tea of the month, daily proper tea and lunch and always have available a quarterly events' calendar and promotions to keep the customer interested and entertained. They also take information to their friends, co-workers and family.

Other special events we have held are fashion shows to promote our large-sized women's clothing line, floral demonstrations and "Tea Talks."

PERSONAL CONTACTS

One of the first things you should do to promote your business at the on-set is to begin making a list of every person, church, club, employee group and any other contacts you know or have a connection. A list needs to be started early because as you think about your contacts and others will come to mind. Think of everyone you know and solicit their help in coming up with people who would like to receive your mailings and promotions. This list will form the basis of your initial customer base. Also, go to the library and ask for an on-line list of all the women's clubs, women's associations and churches in your area and print the list for mailing your newsletter.

We suggest that you plan a special private event immediately after your opening, one that is a private affair for friends and contacts. Also, don't forget your neighbors where you live. We place a full page flyer in our local neighborhood newsletter and simply pay for postage or printing. Again, use your imagination to promote your initial event.

When you hold your private event for friends and associates plan a program that will initiate referrals. Develop a "Free Gift" form to collect referrals. You will tell your guests that their referrals will be invited to your grand opening. This will be the beginning of your marketing efforts.

DIRECT MAIL CARDS

One of the least expensive methods of consistently promoting your business will be the use of post cards. We use a larger six by nine card for promotion when we need room to give details. We use the smaller four by five card if we are promoting a single event. Direct mail cards take less postage, labor and save you money to print. You can use a picture postcard of your tea room to get the recipients immediate attention. Colored pictures are more expensive, but there are national companies that offer specials periodically and you can take advantage of these special prices to print a large supply of cards.

Using a colorful card with pictures of your business provides you with a low cost way to purchase a mailing list and mail directly to affluent women, churches and clubs in your area. The card mailer is an excellent choice for continually promoting your business and we have found direct mailers work best for marketing.

MAILING LISTS

We periodically purchase affluent women mailing lists for the key zip codes in our area and send them a direct mail card or our newsletter. The newsletter is usually three pages – double sided or six full pages of information about our business. The newsletter offers a better opportunity to communicate the uniqueness of our business. We use colored pictures of the inside and outside of our tea room that we take with a digital camera. Microsoft word has a good two-column or three-column page layout for newsletters. This is one of the best ways to market to your targets and to customers because it allows you to tell your story.

CUSTOMER MAILING LIST

As your customer base begins to grow, you will want to do a monthly or bi-monthly newsletter or events direct mail card to your customer base. <u>Your customers will be your absolute best marketing support team if you have designed a unique tea room and gift gallery that provides gifts and a very comfortable and inviting dining experience.</u> That is – if your food is good!

To collect your customer names and addresses you will want to purchase a nice guest book and train your staff to always encourage the customer to sign the guest book. You may also get guest names by having a monthly drawing and giving each guest the card to complete when the hostess is seating them. *<u>Never, never, never fail to have an effective system for collecting guests mailing addresses and always train your staff to promote the guest book and monthly drawing.</u>* You may even want to place a picture of this month's drawing on the card. To comply with the new privacy laws you may want to place a notice that you adhere to all privacy laws in fine print at the bottom of the card.

BROCHURES

We have not heavily used brochures except for catering events and special group promotions. We use the brochure to hand to people who ask for information. The brochure can be designed by an artist or you can use desk top publishing and pull some clip art off the web to develop your brochure. We also have a carry-out menu available for local customers.

When developing your brochure you need to include information on who, what, when where and how – regarding the theme of your brochure and include your name, phone number, email, web site (if any) and your fax number.

BUSINESS CARDS

Another item we have not been very concerned with are business cards because there is no room to promote your business on a business card. The best use for your business card is to give to church group leaders or contacts you meet in public so they have some way to contact you later. Be sure to print your Email address and web address on the card in addition to other pertinent information.

Your business card should carry your logo and all printed material should coordinate with your image and identity. Make sure all printed material is consistent and matches your colors and image.

Your business cards may be done on your computer if you can do desk top publishing and scan on a piece of clip art to add interest to your card. If you are the "Painted Lady" (which means a Victorian house) you may want a line art sketch of your house, or you may choose the Victorian era or English theme and use angels or other Victorian clip art images to carry your theme into all printed material including your business cards. Just use your own judgment if you are a writer or designer. If not, seek a designer to properly communicate your desired image.

MAILING LISTS

Mailing lists are easy to find for your initial promotions and mailings. You can get on the Internet and use search engines by typing in the words, "mailing list companies" and shop for companies to check out. The criteria we use in the Central Ohio area is:

- Affluent women list with assets of over $250,000. You need a large metropolitan area when you use a high net worth specification. The idea is to market to mature women in your market area.
- Select the zip codes that are more middle-to-upper scale or financially successful communities.

- Since women's groups travel quite a distance to visit various tea rooms, you may also want to target women's clubs and churches in other zip codes in your state. We have women's groups from all over the state visit us regularly.

- Target your market within a 50 mile radius

Two list companies we have used for purchasing mailing lists are:

CIS - 612 Corporate Way, Valley Cottage, NY 10989, (800) 547-list
Fax: 845-268-7629/ Email: CIS@CISMarketing.com Web Site: cismarketing.com

American Lists - 88 Orchard Road, CN 529, Princeton, NJ 08543
(800) 252-5478 (888) 830-5478 Ext. 3022 Fax: (908) 874-4433
Email: list@amlist.com Web site: www.amlist.com

You will also need to inform the list company how you want to receive the list. Do you want it on a disk, on labels and a disk, do you want multiple use or one time use and do you want a printed copy with phone numbers. We suggest that you have Act II or other mailing software that is compatible with the company list format so that you can put the names on your computer for future mailings.

As you send out mailings to your list you will find some are returned due to people moving. Keep all returns and delete the names from your list as they come in so that you don't pay for future mailings that are wasted.

The number of people you regularly mail to will depend on your market area and the size of your business. We suggest that the market area and population for your city and county be no less than 100,000 for a small tea room business, 250,000 plus for a medium sized business and 500,000 to one million plus for a large tea room, a large size women's clothing line, large gift gallery and seating for 70 – 100 people for your tea room.

We suggest that your mailing list be a minimum of 2,000 names to launch your business and would encourage your first few mailings of your newsletter to be 5,000 – 10,000 names. It takes time to get your business off the ground and the more you promote during your initial first year launch, the sooner you can get customer referrals working to grow your business. <u>Don't neglect the marketing of your business if you want it to succeed.</u> Make sure your email, web site and other pertinent information is always included in all print material.

Display ads can be used periodically to keep your name in front of the local audience or used in the yellow pages so that new people can find you. We do not use a lot of classified or display ads to promote our business. We have found it to be an expensive way to find new customers, however we do use display ads to maintain our community image.

The following media resources have been used for display ads to get our name in front of different readers:
- Local city newspapers
- Antique publications
- Specials in state magazines
- Local yellow pages

CO-OPERATIVE MARKETING

We have also gone to local businesses that are similar to ours such as bed-and-breakfasts, antique shops, gift shops, etc. and offered to take the time to do a joint newsletter that we all shared in the cost to produce and mail. The co-op opportunity will vary in our own area and we found some small businesses are very backwards and do not understand the value of a co-op marketing effort to reduce everyone's marketing costs. However, don't be surprised if you find local business owners don't get the value of cooperative marketing.

The advantage of co-op marketing is that each business can hand out the co-op marketing newsletter or flyer to all of their customers and promote each other's business to customers. It also allows you to purchase a much larger mailing list and reach a broader audience in your market areas.

Promoting this idea will take preparation. You must do a sample layout of your marketing piece or newsletter to show the general marketing idea. We have found that many business owners are their own worst enemy and don't seem to be creative thinkers. You will also need to work up a cost sheet for the project for mailing list cost, postage and printing. Set a target of five to seven businesses that you can persuade to join in your marketing effort. If you are not a "sales person" you will not get this idea off the ground. You have to show fellow business owners the benefits. It takes work, but so does any marketing effort. Cutting marketing costs can be a big benefit by trading some work effort to share marketing costs. *Attached is an example of one of our co-op efforts.*

NEWSPAPER INSERTS

We use inserts to replace most display ads when using the local newspapers. An insert will be loose in the paper and can be extracted and kept for future reference. You can also use an 8½" by 11" size insert and get more content than you could in an expensive display ad.

You can insert a menu, special event, promote monthly teas and almost any activity you wish by completing a newspaper insert. We feel you get a lot more for your money than you can with a display ad. Usually your local newspaper can select certain sections of their delivery area to insert so that you can target market to the more affluent areas of the readership. Talk to your local paper advertising department to see how they can sort areas for doing an insert. This will save you a lot of money. Your insert will also serve as a mailer, a page in your next newsletter or may be handed out to customers. It can serve a number of marketing functions.

Don't forget also that you may be able to insert your newsletter or at least a condensed version of your newsletter into your paper as well. Check with your local paper to see if they can insert multiple page inserts or if they only accept single sheets. Discuss with them the size, folding requirements, etc. in order to make your decision regarding newspaper inserts.

CHAMBER OF COMMERCE SUPPORT

Your local Chamber may be pro-active or ineffective. Many communities don't properly fund their chamber budget and they hire uncreative people to staff their chamber. You will want to visit your chamber to evaluate all the opportunities offered in your specific community.

The first thing the chamber will want you to do is join. That may or may not be worthwhile depending on how pro-active your chamber is in promoting local businesses. Ask for their business promotion activities designed to specifically help small businesses in their community to see if joining is worthwhile. The progressiveness and vision of the Chamber president is the key to the benefits of the local Chamber of Commerce. In the city were we live, 85 percent of the chamber budget goes for community social activities, not business promotion. They have missed their mission. The Chamber of Commerce is supposed to be a pro-active support organization for businesses, but most of the people hired have never run a business. What a shame!

It reminds us of a speech Dr. Kenneth McFarlane gave before the national Chamber of Commerce. Dr. McFarlane stated that he was hired by a New England area Chamber of Commerce back in the days of the building of bomb shelters to research if their area should build bomb shelters for their citizens. He did local research and talked to a number of community leaders and gave his report to the local chamber. Dr. McFarlane told the local chamber that they did not need a bomb shelter program because his visit with numerous local community leaders told him that the local chamber had, **"successfully repelled everything headed their way for over 20 years!"**

Our advice regarding your local chamber is to visit their office and explore all the services they provide to determine if they could help you. Here are some of the potential opportunities in our local area that are available through the chamber:

- Business listing in the Chamber Directory
- Promotion opportunities to new residents/businesses
- Chamber after hours events
- Ribbon cutting for your open house event
- Special luncheons and dinners
- Real estate new homes & a welcome gift package

PROPERTY SIGNS

Your business location should be in a high traffic area, whether it be on a busy street or in a very active shopping mall. We have stayed away from malls because a new mall development tends to wipe out business from an older mall. Customers are very fickle when it comes to loyalty to a specific mall…if a bigger and better mall is built, chances are the customers will go there. The rich man, woman or corporation that has the money to build a mega mall can quickly destroy another, smaller mall's business. For this reason we will only describe street signs because a mall will have its own sign code to follow.

Our Victorian house is located within two blocks of the main uptown area of Marysville, Ohio. We are on the busiest thoroughfare coming off the State Route 33 freeway. The exit from the freeway is State Route 36, which becomes 5th street where we are located. We are exactly one mile from the exit and are easily accessible. We have over 15,000 cars each day driving by our business. The local traffic is a valuable marketing tool for us. Our signage is incredibly important, so we have designed an attractive, colorful and easy to read version of an old- fashioned sign.

If you locate your business on a busy street, your sign will need to be simple, direct and have large print so that people driving by can read it. If the letters are too small, they will never see the words.

In our city we cannot have a sign on the street that has more than 12 square feet and must be no more than one foot off the ground. We have a corner lot at 5th and Oak and could have two signs if the signs could be 500 feet apart, but we don't have 500 feet between the two street areas. So we have one sign on 5th street. Our first sign was a mistake. It was professional and looked great but the words were too small to be read by traffic driving by. So we changed it to a very few words that included our name, restaurant, tea room & gifts. This allowed us to build a sign so that we could make the words very large so drivers could quickly read the sign on their way by our tea room. We also had to add the word "restaurant" along with out tea room sign because it will shock you how many people really don't know what a tea room is.

We also found that the word tea room may eliminate men from coming in for lunch or dinner because many "men" have the image that a tea room is for "women." So we used the word everyone is familiar with – restaurant along with tea room and gift gallery to avoid this perception. The fact is that we have men executives, judges, lawyers, etc. come in and they are always surprised by the quantity and quality of our food. They also find that they can buy nice gifts at a reasonable price without all the shopping hassle. Men often hate to shop in the local store and love our assistance and beautiful, free gift wrapping.

To develop your sign we suggest that you first visit your local and city administrative office to find out what is required in the area, what zoning laws are required and who to see for details. You will also want to find out how to file for a variance hearing if the signage laws will not accommodate the type and color of sign you wish to use.

Next you will want to design a sign that is professional. You can tour the area for ideas and then rough out your own before using a professional. Make sure your sign image coordinates with your overall business image and color scheme. Since we use a Victorian & English theme, we use the Victorian area colors such as burgundy and teal.

Your final step will be to contact local sign companies that do commercial signs and get them to bid on your project. We don't use neon signs because they are too modern and commercial. Also, neon signs are very expensive. We use wooden signs painted in our colors and underground flood lighting to keep the cost down. We suggest that you shop several sign companies for price.

BILLBOARDS

Affordability is the issue when considering a street or freeway billboard. We found our freeway billboard to bring in a lot of guests, especially during the summer months and the sign continually reminds travelers you are still in town. If cost is an obstacle, you may be able to share a sign with another similar business. We shared with another local gift shop.

When using a billboard you only have a brief time to impact your message. You will need to be a person of "few words" (up to 10 only) to make the sign effective. For example, you may only want to state that you are a 'TEA ROOM" and/or a "GIFT GALLERY" and restaurant. Work with a designer or the billboard company to come up with ideas that will get your message across clearly and quickly. We recommend billboards if you can afford the monthly cost of $500-$1,500. If you locate your business in a large city or resort area, costs could be much higher. Billboards are a consistent way to remind people about your business.

GIFT WRAPPING AS A MARKETING TOOL

Most stores do not gift wrap and it is difficult to get free gift wrapping for the Christmas season. We have found that free gift wrapping can be a great marketing tool. We carefully select quality gift wrap, tissue paper, and colorful gift bags and ribbons. One of our best marketing tools for gift wrapping is making very colorful bows and using a large gold printed label of our Victorian house on the package.

Why do we use a nice label? Because the gift may be going to a new prospective customer and if you do a really quality job of gift wrapping they will be impressed at the quality of your business. As a small business, this is one of the ways you can be unique and stand out from the competition. Don't under estimate the value of an excellent gift wrapping service. Customers will be proud to give such a lovely wrapped gift and the recipient will be impressed. This service is a great marketing tool for your business even though it is an expensive business service. It is another way you can be unique. We have even had customers want us to wrap gifts from other places because they like our wrapping so much. Of course, we say no or we charge for the service.

MARKET, MARKET, MARKET

Your business will not get off the ground or survive unless you place a lot of value on marketing. Your start-up budget must support a strong marketing effort until you have customers standing in line. We have given you a number of effective marketing examples in this guide. This by no means is all the marketing alternatives you have available. Church fundraising, sponsoring local charities, providing a Christmas tree fully decorated at a local hospital auction and other things can be done to promote your business. When our tree won the "People's Choice" award, it was published in the paper.

We have received free TV coverage but have not mentioned television advertising. We have not been able to afford TV advertising. However, if we had time we would develop a local cable half-hour tea room program that would discuss food, health, Victorian era, English customs and other topics of interest to women. We would, but we just do not have the time to do it. Television is the most powerful media and also the most expensive. Use it if you can afford to penetrate your market with local television spots, especially after you are established and have everything "prettied up" so that you can show off your business on TV.

Never under estimate the value of using several marketing, public relations and image alternatives to promote your business because they all work together. Be on the lookout for events you can use to promote your business. Always use direct mail during the early phases of your business and always consistently promote to your client mailing list. We have strongly encouraged you about the need to promote your business. Without a well planned marketing program, your business may not survive in this competitive world.

DEVELOPING YOUR WEB SITE

WHY USE A WEB SITE?

Many people misunderstand how a business uses the Internet and a web site to promote their business, because of the **"get rich promotion schemes"** you see in direct mail, on TV and in books and promotional material. Some people do make a living on the Internet marketing produces and services, how-to booklets and gift baskets on E-Bay. ***Making money on the Internet is not the topic of this section.*** The purpose of this discussion regarding having a web site for your business is to provide you with the basics of how you can use this valuable tool as you would any other marketing tool.

First of all, if you haven't visited our web site at www.A-TEA-ROOM.com you may want to take a tour. *Our web site **was not** professionally designed.* We developed it as a customer service and to allow people to look us over to see if they want to visit us. There is no real quality design on our web site.

Why should you have a web site? It reminds us of the story of a company executive and marketing officer that were meeting and the marketing director said, "We need a web site." The president asked what the cost would be and the marketing director said, "About a million dollars!" The president then asked the question, ***"Why do we need a million dollar web site?"*** To which the marketing director stated, "Because everyone has one!"

You need a web site if you are serious about building a business and expect guests to visit you from greater distances for the following reasons:
- To get a map to your place
- Take a virtual tour of your tea room to decide if it is a good place to visit
- Show friends a nice place and to help friends promote other friends
- Provide information about your business
- Make your business available 24/7
- Promote events
- Post your menu and menu changes
- Promote an online newsletter

Your web site does not need all the "stuff" and links we have on our site. We don't find the other shopping sites effective at all. The only real information you need on your site are your menus, pictures of your beautiful tea room, directions, times open, promotions of group events, special teas, contact information and other promotions and activities. Keep it simple, direct and to the point. Tell your story so people all over the area can visit you to decide if they want to come to tea at your place.

WEB SITE IMAGE

Your web site can be very basic to allow interested parties to tour your business on-line. If you don't have a gift gallery you can add an online shopping feature to add additional sales. Your image can be simple or sophisticated. Our site is designed to be easily understood, but has little design. We use pictures of our facility to show off our image. Pictures of the Red Hat Society, The Ohio Victorian Tea Society and other photo opportunities will promote your facility well if you have used strong colors that will "pop" out at you in photo form. Pictures allow you to pass through your business image and theme without having to design an on-line image if you want to save on costs.

To keep cost down for promoting your tea room, get a digital camera and take your own pictures. Make sure they show case your tea room well or your image will turn people away. We use the type of digital camera with the small disk and software that allows us to take a picture and copy it over to a CD or disk to take to the web master. By the way, shop around for a web master because prices vary a great deal. Stay away from the big web producers because they usually charge big fees to large companies. We pay $40 an hour for our web master. If someone in your family is capable of using online software to complete a web site, this may be an alternative. Just make sure your pictures show well and sell your image appropriately.

Keeping your site simple to use and displaying pictures is a low-cost way to set up a site. **However, be careful with pictures because some people are still on the "slow" telephone Internet access lines and pictures can take too long to come up on the screen**. People will get discouraged and leave the site. We have a few pictures on the home page, but most of the pictures are on secondary pages so your home page can come up more quickly and then the visitors can select the pictures later on in the tour. Your menu, map and other important information should be immediately available to visitors.

ADDING ON-LINE SHOPPING

On-line shopping is not necessary for your site. Simply having a basic web site is like an informational brochure that is available 24 hours a day, seven days a week…this is a valuable marketing tool.

However, if you do wish to add on-line shopping to build a second income over the next few years, there are several ways to go. Many wholesale companies will allow you to download pictures to your site from their catalog inventory. Drop shipment companies will sell you a web site that provides total on-line shopping with credit cards.

Be careful when adding on-line shopping that you select quality merchandise or this service could hurt your business. One of our web sites is with SMC, a national merchandising company that drop ships and has been around for years. You may visit their web site at www.smcorp.com. They have three levels of web sites that offer hundreds of gift products. Their quality varies and some merchandise does not fit your image, but there are enough gifts to give the shopper a wide variety of choices. The key is not to clutter up your site with too many things. I think we have done just that as we learned how to use the Internet. Some of the things on our site may or may not be useful.

One disadvantage to adding on-line shopping is that it will complicate your site more if you use wholesale vendor's pictures because you will have to constantly be changing and replacing merchandise pictures. Discuss this option with various wholesalers listed in the back of this manual if on-line shopping is of interest to you. One advantage to having merchandise on-line is that relatives and friends who live in other states who come in while visiting family members or on business trips can stay in touch with you and will allow you to gradually build up an on-line business. Don't count on making money on the Internet with a store web site unless you strongly emphasize this aspect of your business regularly and it will still take a lot of time to realize income from your site.

A web site needs instructions for ordering for both your store directly and for on-line merchandise. You will need privacy policy, shipping costs, gift wrapping instructions and other information. Visit our site and others to print off copies to study as you think about this aspect of your business.

You could begin adding your own gift baskets and packaging items for sale from your own work during slow times. Selling packages of teas mixed with gifts and other items can begin small and grow over time. But, never fail to offer a gift coupon on-line so that a family member or friend can purchase a coupon for others. Coupons are a great marketing tool to meet new customers.

To learn more about other web site in your type of business, go to a search engine on the web and type in key words such as tea rooms, English tea rooms, Victorian tea rooms, gift shops, etc. to get a feel of what is being done by your competitors.

WEB SITE COSTS

The cost of a web site can be minimal, however we do not recommend the free sites that you can find available because they are loaded with banners, advertising and tracking devices to identify customer e-mails. Talk to friends and contacts about who they use locally or nationally.

The first thing you will have to do is reserve a name for your web site and to do that you have to have an Internet provider to host the address you choose. We choose A-TEA-ROOM.com so we could get in the "A" section of the alphabet. You cannot use "A" on the Google search engine but there are ways to list your tea room categories in six or seven ways to get multiple listings. We recommend checking out Google to control how your tea room is listed when you establish a web site.

Once you have a name and a host Internet provider you will need a web master to set up your web site. Do not count on all web masters to be designers, too. They are usually not designers. If you go to a larger web company they will have a staff that includes technicians and designers but they are expensive. Check around in your local area to find good designers and a web programmer that will be inexpensive, unless you have the funds to go all out.

As stated before, we pay $40 per hour for technical programming to our web master and do our own layout. He has absolutely no design skills and if you visit our site you will see that we don't have great skills either. Our web site was simply developed to be very personable to our customers and to provide access to information throughout the USA wherever our customers live.

We also pay an Internet provider hosting fee of $102 per quarter. An additional fee will be your name reservation fee with Network Solutions where we protect our online name. The annual renewal fee is $35 or less.

Costs for buying marketing rights to ready-made on-line shopping web sites such as SMC can vary. Do a lot of looking before making a decision. We pay SMC an annual membership fee of $195 and paid

$795 for the right to add their on-line gift shopping mall. There is also a $29 monthly maintenance fee. These costs can be expensive, but they allow you to add a service for your customers who live too far away and who may wish to purchase from your store of on-line to get a gift for someone. We do not suggest this is a priority up front. This facet of your business can be added later, after you are more established.

BUSINESS OPERATIONS

STAFFING AND TRAINING

Owning a small business does not allow you the luxury of hiring highly skilled labor. We have found that people who apply for work and who claim to have a lot of skills bring with them two problems. **Number one,** they are not as teachable and, **number two,** they are too expensive for a small tea room and gift gallery business. So what has our own experience taught us in seeking good help?

The first thing we look for when hiring is attitude. Is the prospective employee eager to work? Will they stay after your hire them and are they willing to learn? If they are willing to learn and have a positive attitude, this is most important. New hires that have little experience are wonderful trainees because they want to learn and are grateful for the opportunity. Always lavish positive strokes and encouragement to your staff because they are vital to your business and its success.

Our full time chef quit because she was afraid of failure. She had never worked outside the home and had little confidence. When she threatened to quit in a phone message we called her back and told her we were not going to accept her resignation and we told her to get ready for work because we were coming to pick her up. We trusted and believed in her. She has worked every day since and is vital to our business. We took her in, gave her a lot of strokes, taught her the business and believed in her ability to do the job. She is a wonderful and loyal person. She will protect our business as if it were here own because we treated her with respect, never talked down to her and proved our faith in her by giving her responsibility and allowing her to make mistakes in the early stages of working with us. Now she is our chef and we are very happy with her work, but it took patience, time and a lot of positive strokes. We hired her because she had a willingness to learn and did what we asked of her. She had the right attitude to be taught.

Your best source of finding good people can be from your own customers. Listen to them when they tell you about a friend, daughter or grandchild that needs work or is not happy with their current work. Keep your eyes and ears open for people who may be a candidate for a good employee.

Consistent training with hands-on show and tell techniques on an almost daily basis will help get an unskilled employee up and running quickly. Showing confidence in them and encouraging them regularly will build their confidence and you will see them bloom into a confident and friendly hostess, waitress and employee doing whatever is required of them.

We are fortunate to have a daughter with exceptional business management skills. We have exposed her to our businesses since she was very young. Therefore, she is confident and can be assertive and is an excellent problem solver. She is left in charge when we vacation or have a health problem. We never have to worry about the business because we have competent, honest, dependable employees who care about us.

In summary, we do not try to hire people who think they are the best and the brightest because they expect too much and will not stay with you. We hire people we can train, compliment them almost daily and show our gratitude with strokes, thanks and surprise bonuses. These very personal recognitions tell the employees we care, we believe in and like them. This will mean more than money to people who want to do something in life but never get the chance for one reason or another. In a small business, you will want to cross-train all the employees to fill in for each other in all the daily business activities. This will give them greater confidence in themselves and provide back up when someone gets sick or can't make it to work.

Absentee business owners and larger tea rooms and gift galleries will need to hire a more experienced and trained manager that has the right background working in a similar business. A larger business requires more skills and would not operate as well without a trained staff or someone who can take charge daily and manage the employees on a daily basis. At this point, our current staff is so well trained that they could run a much larger facility.

PLANNING EMPLOYEE JOB DESCRIPTIONS

With our small business, we as owners and our daughter and chef basically run the day-to-day operations. We require a very small staff. We have one chef and we have cross trained other employees as back up. We all do whatever is necessary during busy periods. The chef's husband does handyman work occasionally when things need done such as mowing the lawn, minor repairs, changing filters, etc.

The following will provide an outline of our current staff's job functions:

- **Head Cook & Kitchen Manager**
  - Cook daily (lunch & tea) manage and help in the preparation of gourmet dinners and for special promotions such as a grill out.
  - Create new menus and attractive presentations as inspired.
  - Prepare special orders of customers such as menu dishes, decorated cakes, etc.
  - Assist owners in planning/operating carry-out functions of the kitchen.
  - Manage the service flow and staff of food preparation.
  - Oversee the ordering and stocking of food and supplies to be purchased for the kitchen's operation.
  - See that the kitchen is kept clean and assist with that duty.
  - Work with owners to improve operations, making suggestions as needed in areas that could cut costs or be enhanced.
  - Oversee the requirements that the Health Dept. dictates informing the owners when issues need to be addressed.
  - See that quality, cleanliness, freshness and presentation of food is always at its best.
  - Assist with any kitchen or service task (food service or retail) that is vital to the efficiency of the business operation.
  - Inform owners of any problems or potential problems before they escalate.
  - Let owners know if there is a time available or a desire to help with the retail or serving side of the business.

- **Management Assistant & Kitchen Manager Assistant**
  - Assist Kitchen Coordinator with all kitchen assignments as needed. Assist with daily (lunch & tea) menus and help in the preparation of gourmet dinners and for special promotions such as grill outs.
  - Help with the service flow of food preparation.
  - See that the kitchen is kept clean and assist with that duty.
  - Wash dishes, help bus the dirty dishes on busy days and assist with any task that improves efficiency and timeliness.
  - Work with owners to improve operations making suggestions as needed in areas that could be enhanced or that would cut costs.
  - See that quality, cleanliness, freshness and presentation of food is always at its best.

- o Inform owners of any problems or potential problems before they escalate.
- o Let owners know if there is a time available or a desire to help with the retail or serving side of the business.
- o Assist with any kitchen or service task (food service or retail) that is vital to the efficiency of the business operation.

- **Hostess**
  - o Greet customers with a warm smile, socialize and seat customers
  - o Assist with cleaning tables
  - o Assist with the cash register

- **Server**
  - o Be responsible, dependable, customer relations person, can work under pressure, can carry out the directions of management and handle numerous and varied tasks, accurate and strong attention to customer needs and details.
  - o Prepare and set tables for lunch and other dining activities.
  - o Take food orders and serve food.
  - o Act as expeditor for keeping food service timely and efficient.
  - o Assist dining room manager with assignments as directed such as water, coffee or tea preparation.
  - o See that beverage and soup service areas are kept clean and stocked.
  - o Wash dishes in beverage or kitchen area as needed, when kitchen staff member(s) is absent or when time is available.
  - o Take turns carrying dirty dishes to the kitchen when kitchen staff is busy or under staffed.
  - o Dust, sweep or perform cleaning and organizing as requested.
     See that quality, cleanliness and presentation of food is always at its best.
  - o Assist with any kitchen or service task (food service or retail) that is vital to the efficiency of the business operation.
  - o Inform owners of any problems or potential problems before they escalate.
  - o Let owners know if there is a time available or a desire to help with the kitchen side of the business.

These job functions basically complete our tea room and gift gallery staffing requirements. The larger your business is – the more people you will need to fill these roles. Our business is small, housed in a 103 year old Victorian farm house with about 3000 square feet of space. We seat 40 customers for lunch and in the summer we can seat 40 more customers on the deck on a nice day. An absentee owner would need more staff and a larger business would also require more staff. Your requirements will be based on the size of the business you establish.

The hostess is our daughter or one of the servers. They welcome guests, encourage them to sign the guest register for mailings and assist them in being seated. We normally have two servers and the chef and hostess during rush periods.

All of us help with cleaning, doing dishes, keeping the kitchen spotless and dusting. However, our daughter is an excellent and detailed cleaner and is great at keeping the store polished. She is also excellent with the customers.

REFUND POLICY

We do not give refunds. The reason for this is that we have had people bring back doilies that are soiled and used, cloths that have perspiration stains and other ridiculous situations. Cash flow is so important that it really puts a strain on a small business to refund money unless state laws require a refund of merchandise – typically within three days from the date of purchase.

START-UP BUDGET

Planning your business is one of the most important steps in the process of starting a business. The less experience you have in the business you are thinking of starting the more time and research you must invest to make certain you have thought of everything necessary to successfully own and operate a business.

The first rule in developing a start-up budget is once you have reached what you feel is your total start-up costs for the first year, you will then double your estimates. Another rule for your start-up budget is to combine your first year of start-up and ongoing operating budget together in the start-up budget for your first year. The first year will be a start-up period.

If you feel your business will cost $50,000 to start and operate for the first year, you will allocate $100,000 to be safe because Murphy's Law will always be present. You will not normally think of everything that will be required and not everything will go according to plans. If you have estimated that your monthly fixed and variable overhead costs will be $9,000, plan to double that estimate for the first year. It is the first year that most surprises will show up and you must have enough money to get you through these surprises – because you will have surprises on costs.

The following pages provide you a sample start-up budget for a small, medium and large business. It includes the tea room and gift gallery budgets to develop, open and run a sample business for the first year. <u>The model budget we have provided is an example only and we do not present this information as being accurate for your own budget because costs will vary depending upon the cost of living in your area and costs will vary depending on your own ability to set up a business, the research you do and the funds you have available.</u> We warn you to seek competent advice and get a second opinion regarding your own start-up budget.

Review the attached sample start-up budget. The small model is based upon our own experience when we purchased our Victorian house and installed the tea room and gift gallery. Again, we present this start-up budget model as an example only and in no way do we imply what your experience will be.

Example: The Victorian Painted Lady, LLC monthly budget

(Rounded to the nearest dollar)

Electric	675 average
Gas	315
Phone	250
Water/sewage/trash	250
Alarm system	18
Fire alarm system	25
Prop/liability ins.	275
Maintenance	120
Bank services/cc interest	150
Postage	120
Printing/menus/fliers	120
Wages	600
Food	2,000
Supplies	300
Misc.	500
TOTAL	$6,718

POTENTIAL PROFIT

FOLLOWING A ONE-YEAR START-UP PERIOD IN A CITY WITH A POPULATION OF AT LEAST 500,000, YOU COULD EXPECT THE FOLLOWING FINANCIAL RESULTS.

Type of Business:	English Tea Room & Gift Gallery		
Expected Gross Income Profile:	**LOW**	**AVERAGE**	**HIGH**
	$150,000	**$250,000**	**$500,000**
Average Start-Up Investment:	**$125,000**	**$350,000**	**$600,000**
Stability:	**Moderate**		

Risk Factor – Start-up Phase:	**High**
Risk Factor – On-going:	**Moderate**
Tea Industry Growth Prospects:	**Excellent**
Absentee Ownership Potential:	**Good, with strong leadership/management**

NOTE: This report is based upon the average population of a typical middle class American city. Smaller towns may require a more modest start-up investment and larger cities may require much more capital. Also, costs will vary greatly based upon the area of the United States you plan to start your business. Another major variable is whether you intend to buy a current restaurant, buy and remodel a building or simply lease a building in a great location. You are warned that these financials will vary, depending upon where you are locating your business and the business choices you make. Our report does not address establishing a major tea room and gift gallery complex in a large new shopping mall or purchasing an expensive commercial property that could cost from one to four million dollars. Obviously, investors with a large amount of capital can do anything they wish to do with the idea of a tea room and gift gallery. Your gift inventory alone in a large complex could be as much as one million dollars. However, for the purposes of this guide, we are focused on the average costs for an average would-be tea room investor with a small amount of capital. Obviously the choices you make will determine your budget.

GENERAL BUSINESS PRINCIPLES

Running a business is not easy. Everything you can imagine will happen to you as you develop your business. We have the highest regard for anyone who has successfully built a business because it took a lot of guts, confidence, ingenuity and worked very hard.

To run a business you must be an independent thinker because you will be required to come up with solutions to problems. It has been said that people who are successful simply have the ability to, "Solve more problems than the rest of the population!"

Owning and operating a business requires marketing savvy, good people skills and financial management. That is why we placed at the very beginning of this manual a self-assessment section to

95

assist you in evaluating your own skills and abilities to see if you feel you should even consider running your own business. If you get discouraged easily, you will fail because a business will sometimes "beat your emotions to death." If you are not creative you may fail to come up with the right solutions to your business. The bottom line to owning and operating a business is that you must have what is called, "staying power" to survive the first few years of a business start-up phase. If you are determined to start your own business, you may need to consider partners to fill in the gaps or you may not have what it takes to survive in your own business.

The most common business failure factors are:

- Lack of capital
- Insufficient experience
- Inability to hire and manage people
- No marketing experience
- Lack of entrepreneurial drive
- No patience and perseverance
- Overly optimistic expectations
- No training in the business you are about to create
- Failure to stick to your business plan

FINANCING YOUR BUSINESS

METHODS OF FINANCING YOUR BUSINESS

<u>The first warning we will give you in financing your business is that you should never take on too much short-term debt.</u> Monthly payments can become a rope around your neck if the business gets off the ground too slowly. Ideally you would be better off with no monthly mortgage payments or loan payments but that is not always realistic. Just remember that your business may not create the income required to make loan payments during the start-up period.

The first source of capital however, should always be your own funds or loan sources. The easiest and quickest way to get started is from your own resources and you will then own the entire business and not have to work with a financial partner or give up part of your equity for financing. Mortgaging a property for capital is a good source of funds, especially in a low interest environment. If you think you have enough money to start your business it is still a good idea to open a second mortgage credit line just in case more capital is needed.

If you find that you do not have enough money to live on and finance a business you will have to drop the idea or seek other sources of funding.

FRIENDS, FAMILY AND CONTACTS

Ideally the best choice to eliminate debt payments is to determine how much capital you have and how much you will require to finance your business the first year. Then you will complete a well planned business plan to present to friends, family members and contacts. You will not go to them initially asking them for money. You will go to them and ask for their help in reviewing your business plan and to see if they can find holes in the plan.

One word of warning when you do this is that you must realize friends and family will most likely try to discourage you. Very few of the people you know will want you to succeed. It seems to be human nature to be destructive of your ideas rather than positive about what you want to do. So, expect negative feedback, but hope some of your contacts have business experience and will give you constructive ideas and serve as an objective critic.

Once you have gone through the process of giving all your contacts your business plan and have asked for their thoughts and sat down with them at lunch to discuss their thoughts, you will then finalize your plan and revise it using any constructive ideas your contacts have provided that make sense.

Next, you will take the plan back to them and show them the final plan developed from their input. Your goal for the next phase of your funding efforts will be to review your start-up budget, tell them that you have $_____ and that you are short $_____. You will now ask each of your contacts if they know anyone who would be interested in being a business partner (active or preferably a silent partner). ***You will ask your contacts for referrals of people who are looking for a business opportunity***. Do not attempt to get them involved. They will ask to be involved if they are interested in your project.

What you are looking for is someone with money to invest as a silent partner and you would be asking to share an equity interest in your tea room. You can look for people who are in the business such as a chef or a manager of a similar business. Even if they don't have the money they may be able to get the money to join you.

When you find a financial partner who is willing to take a piece of the equity in business you have eliminated loan payments and monthly payments to acquire capital. You may also wish to find a working partner to help fill in the gaps in your own personal experience.

To attract a financial partner, you will need an exciting "dream", a good financial forecast, start-up and operating budget and you will want to set up an "S" Corporation or a Limited Liability Company (LLC). No one is going to buy into your dream. You must have some real substance to the idea and show strong confidence and leadership when you decide to start a business otherwise no one will believe you are serious. By investing time in research, planning and establishing a company name and a legal entity you will demonstrate your determination to build a business. You will find that most people will not be creative and do not buy into your dream unless you are already turning your dream into a reality.

Women, especially minority women may also have an edge on getting a government or state backed loan by checking with the Small Business Administration (SBA). State and federal programs are available that will back a loan from a bank for certain businesses started by women. You may also call a SCORE office in your area and visit with one of the retired business counselors provided free by SCORE.

To learn more about what the federal government offers women and minority businesses, go to the Google search engine and type in a search for, "Federal programs for women business owners" or Government loans for women". Plan on spending some time researching all the information available on this site:

The most visible loan source is your local bank. Some banks cater to businesses while others are more interested in personal loans. Check the yellow pages for banks that claim to help small businesses. Before you do, have your business plan, business name and a legal entity set up so that you demonstrate the fact that you are serious about your business. While visiting with the banker also ask if they participate in SBA loan guaranteed programs. By law, the SBA cannot make a loan if you can get a loan at the bank. First you must seek a loan with a bank and get declined. The SBA is a loan of last resort. The SBA cannot make certain type of loans and you must prove your business has the potential to succeed. Seek advice from your banker regarding your business plan and loan presentation. The maximum you can borrow from the SBA is $550,000 or the present limit of 90 percent of the funds required.

To deal with most bankers you will need some form of collateral and they will want to look at your monthly income to be sure you can pay the money back. They are not likely to get excited about an untested business plan income forecast without collateral.

Depending on your situation, a bank may consider loaning on real estate, equipment, inventory and accounts receivable. These types of loans use your assets as collateral. Many banks will loan up to 80 percent of the value of the collateral. Make sure you get a loan term as long as possible to minimize monthly payments and to preserve savings for emergency needs. You can always pay the loan off early if your business grows well.

Another short-term funding source will be your vendors and suppliers. Although you will not be able to finance your start-up costs from these sources, they do often have flooring plans or terms for short-term billing periods. Ask each vendor about their payment policy.

The way you work with vendors is to establish a relationship with your first order and show excitement about your business and the potential to sell their merchandise. Ask them about their payment and invoicing policy and identify vendors you feel will work with you.

After you establish a relationship, let's say you have an open house or a special event coming up and you need more merchandise. Simply talk to the vendor and give them an order with a 30 day billing. You will have the extra merchandise for your event and will hopefully be able to make sales from this new merchandise to pay the vendor in 30 days. Use this option carefully and make sure you pay the invoice on time or you will lose the opportunity to get 30 day or longer invoicing. Personally we try not to use 30 day invoicing too often because you may have a down cycle and not have the income to pay for the merchandise and will have to dig up the cash from personal funds. Believe us, you will have those times when your income drops dramatically and you will not know why the customers are not coming in to buy your merchandise.

Credit cards are another source of cash, but an often expensive one. If you use credit cards only do so for temporary reasons. Paying high interest is not a good method of borrowing money. However, a credit card will only require a small payment each month and can help you get merchandise and pay it off over time. Disciplined use of a credit card can be helpful if used wisely.

HAVING STAYING POWER

Your survival in a business is dependent on all the things discussed in this business start-up guide. No one can predict how well you will do. Carefully studying this manual, seeking the help and critique of friends and other sources of advice will be the best investment you can make – ***BEFORE YOU START YOUR BUSINESS!*** Avoid emotional involvement because emotions and excitement about an idea is only the catalyst that helps launch the planning stages of a business. Ideas are a dime-a-dozen and they are worthless unless all the components of a business plan are thoroughly though out and implemented.

In conclusion, the term *"staying power"* is your ability to get through the financial and emotional **"rough times"** so that your business can survive, because there will be **"rough times"** with any business. You will need *"staying power"* when your business hits those unexpected cash flow slumps. You will need *"staying power"* when you are emotionally discourage or down-in-the-mouth.

Typically you will need staying power for five years or longer to really bring the full potential of your business into reality. You will need to have drive and stamina to make it in any small business.

If you have the *"right stuff"* a small business can be exciting, provide you with freedom to use your own brain, be creative, experience life, enjoy great tax deductions, take business trips instead of vacations and live life to the fullest. Never fail to eventually follow your dreams so that when you leave this earth, you will not have to say, *"I wish I could do it all over again!"* That would be a sad thing to hear any human being say. What a shame it would be to go all the way through life working for a jerk or a selfish boss or dream of owning your own business so that you can free yourself from the bondage of working for someone else.

Free your mind a little and dream about owning a beautiful tea room with a gift gallery full of unique and beautiful gifts. Think of serving people healthy teas and wholesome food. Dream of the time when you can welcome customers into a beautiful dinning room with all the trappings of the Victorian and/ or English décor and feel how proud you would be to "show off "your own business – a business you built with your own sweat and effort. It can be an experience far beyond the drudgery of working for someone else who will not listen to your ideas. You will step beyond the 70 percent of Americans who just talk about doing things, but never do anything about their dreams. You will step beyond the followers who work for others and complain, yet never take charge of their life.

Finally, remember the seven steps to success and dream a little. Develop a business plan, ask contacts to give you a critique, do your best to develop your own business – and maybe not now – but eventually your dream will become a reality. In the meantime, learn all you can, gain experience and plan to take control of your future. Don't let life pass you by because you are afraid to try. Complete your business plan and let others tear it apart in order to mature your thoughts and then get going.

OUR CONSULTING SERVICES

The advantage of seeking help in launching a new business is to avoid costly mistakes. Talk to any business owner and they will tell you horror stories of the lessons they have learned with their business. These lessons usually cost a lot of money. The best way to minimize mistakes is to have an experienced person looking over your shoulder as you proceed into a new business.

Yes, we have provided you more information in this manual than you will find anywhere else and it will be very valuable to you. The problem for anyone setting up a tea room for the first time is that they will only get part of the message in this manual because of lack of experience. Experience is the best teacher but it is also the most costly. What you will gain from this manual is tremendous, but a lot of it will be like taking math in school. You learn theory in school but you still have to apply the information to practical application and make the math work on the job. The same is true for anyone studying this manual who has never run a business or who has never operated a gift gallery or restaurant. You will still have to apply all the things in this manual to make if work for you. That is where our experience can help with your individual circumstances. We can save you a lot of time and money.

Our Consulting Services:

Travel expenses will be additional to these prices.

1.   One-two hour consultation at our tea room with lunch: $200

2.   Review of your business plan: $900

3.   Visit your community to review customer base, location
     and provide guidance before beginning: $2,500

4.   Provide public relations consulting for open house, publicity
     promotion and printed image: $2,500

5.   Newsletter design, writing and development: $ 1200

6.   Complete business on-site, marketing and publicity plan: $2900

7.   Normal ongoing hourly consultation: $ 190

8.   Complete one year start-up and launch your business: $30,000
     This program includes a total on-site, hands-on mentoring
     program until you are successfully off the ground.

MISCELLANEOUS EXHIBITS

We have over 50 press releases and feature stories along with samples of our customer newsletters – not inclued.

You may order these if you are interested in getting copies of our 10 years of publicity and marketing material. Price is $16.95

We also sell our proprietary menus and recipes for $99.95.

You may order these by mailing your check to:

Joyce Ann Whitaker & Charles Whitaker

555 Metro Place North, Suite 100

Dublin, Ohio 43017

(800) 800-5720

Anyone considering starting a tea room will save thousands of dollars and hundreds of hours in time and wasted energy by learning from our good and bad experiences running our tea room and gift gallery. Before wasting time and money, hire us to guide you in this exciting new business.

Printed in the United States
24162LVS00002B/203-204

9 781418 428426